Serial

DC's
3 (Rei
   James doug
  (CTW
   Martin Christopher
2 (David cove
   Michael Morgan

Charles Dinwiddie
  Winchester
  David Biddle

beat
Uppingham
Winchester
Malvern
+ Marlborough
in the first
  2/1
3 years in a row

Old Carthusian Golfing Society 1912–2012

A Century of Charterhouse Golf

Nigel Hague
with foreword by Donald Steel

**Old Carthusian Golfing Society 1912–2012:
A Century of Charterhouse Golf**

Copyright © Nigel Hague and Old Carthusian Golfing Society, 2012

The right of Nigel Hague to be identified as the author of this work has been asserted by him in accordance with the Copyright, Designs and Patents Act 1998.

All rights reserved. No part of this book may be reproduced or transferred in any form or by any means, graphic, electronic, or mechanical, including photocopying, recording, taping, or by any information storage retrieval system, without written permission from the author, except for the inclusion of brief quotations in a review.

Every effort has been made to contact and credit the copyright holders of photographs and illustrations.

A catalogue record for this book is available from the British Library.

Designed and produced by Catherine Hollingworth and Pentacor, UK.

ISBN 978-0-9571475-0-8

Printed and bound in Singapore.

First published in the UK in 2012 by Nigel Hague.

Contents

Foreword by Donald Steel	5
Preface	6
Foundation of OCGS	8
The Wreford-Brown family	12
G O Smith	17
Prince Albert of Schleswig-Holstein	18
Horace Hutchinson	20
The Halford Hewitt	
(1) *origins, first tournament, development and captains*	23
(2) *1925–29*	33
(3) *1930–39*	36
(4) *1947–59*	47
(5) *1960–69*	55
(6) *1970–79*	58
(7) *1980–89*	61
(8) *1990–99*	67
(9) *2000–11*	70
The Grafton Morrish	78
The Queen Elizabeth	84
The Bernard Darwin, Senior Darwin and Very Senior Darwin	88
Some Notable Members	93
Halford W Hewitt	93
Ben Travers	96
C V L Hooman	98
J S F Morrison	100
J B Beck	102
T A Bourn	104
H C Longhurst	105
R S Gilbert Scott	106
J E Bayman	108
M J Christmas	110
P J W Benka	112
Secretaries and Treasurers	114
Membership, Meetings and Matches	123
Golf at Charterhouse and the Halford Hewitt golf course	128
Dinners and social events	142
Appendices:	
(1) *Individual Halford Hewitt results*	148
(2) *Halford Hewitt gold medals*	152
(3) *Winners of scratch cups*	152
(4) *OCGS Officers*	154
Author's notes	156
About the Author	157
Index and Acknowledgements	158

Foreword by Donald Steel

Although the founding of the Old Carthusian Golfing Society pre-dates the first playing of the Halford Hewitt by twelve years, one undoubtedly led to the other. The inextricable link was forged because 'Hal' himself was a Carthusian and a fervently patriotic one at that. It is said that early Charterhouse teams treated him with an affectionate lack of respect but he helped sow seeds of a tale that quickly assumed legendary proportions. More importantly, Nigel Hague's admirable Centenary History of the OCGS is welcome proof that the legend lives on. Even so, one of the charms of the author's research is the puncturing of a popular myth as to exactly how Hal's benefaction came about.

No other School can match the OCGS's trademark panache, their colourful approach or the obvious enjoyment they have always derived from simply getting together and playing golf. The outstanding success it has brought may have given ample excuse for celebration but they have never been constrained by results. They are natural fun lovers.

It took Charterhouse a year or two to find their sea(side) legs at Deal, five years, in fact, before they contested a final but, once they had established themselves, their proud dominance was the envy of all. There has been nothing comparable to their seven victories in ten years from 1930 but Charterhouse's legacy to a tournament that has no equal in the world is that their example rubbed off on others. They set the trends.

Of course, none of their successes could have been achieved without a string of fine players – Beck, Bourn, Morrison, Hooman, Longhurst, Bristowe, Scott, Christmas, Hughesdon, and Peter and Mark Benka. However, I must not fall into the trap of conveying the impression that the OCGS's reputation has been solely dependent on the Halford Hewitt. In its heyday, it boasted over 700 members and, in their centenary year, it still has an active fixture list of matches and meetings for like-minded enthusiasts.

Having been involved on the front line as architect, I was well aware of the OCGS's well known generosity that led to the nine-hole golf course at the School in the 1980s. Appropriately christened in honour of Halford Hewitt, it provides the opportunity of spotting stars at an early age but, for those outside the brotherhood, it is also a welcome reminder that Carthusian golfers have always preferred to shape events rather than be carried along by them.

This hard-backed centenary History, assembled by my old friend, Nigel Hague, is another case in point. The first by any Halford Hewitt School Golfing Society to mark a hundred years, it is confirmation that the OCGS do things in style, a style to delight their many friends and admirers. As Chancellors of the Exchequer conclude at the end of Budget speeches (often with far less conviction), "I commend it to you".

Preface

In August 2009, I was asked by Martin Christmas, then the President of the Old Carthusian Golfing Society, if I would consider writing the history of the Society for its centenary in 2012. I was surprised, and at first a little reluctant. For having just completed a similar book for my golf club (Denham), I did not wish to forego the sense of relief and calm which comes to a writer when his book goes off to the printers and there is little further to be done; and also I anticipated that a positive answer might give rise to domestic disapproval. But the flattery inherent in the request, which was repeated shortly afterwards by Roddy Gamble, then the Society's Captain, together with a long-held interest in the subject-matter of such a book, soon caused my reluctance to crumble and so made me hoist the white flag. I have not regretted doing so, as both the research involved and the writing of this book have proved most interesting and enjoyable experiences.

Those who get round to actually reading the earlier parts of the text of this book are likely to be struck by the numerous references to, and quotations from, the writings of Bernard Darwin. I make no apologies for this, for in the opinion of many (including myself) Darwin certainly ranks with the greatest essayists of the 20th century. I first encountered Darwin's writing when I read and re-read my father's copy of his *Golf Between Two Wars*, purchased shortly after its publication in 1944 'in complete conformity with the authorised war economy standards'. At the time, I thought that I was merely reading a golf history, but of course I was falling under the spell of Darwin's incomparable prose. A few years later, I was in a 'hash' (Charterhouse slang for a class) presided over by the great classical scholar and teacher A L 'Uncle' Irvine, when the name of Bernard Darwin came up. "Who is Bernard Darwin?" he asked. I knew that Darwin was 'Our Golf Correspondent' of *The Times*, but an answer involving golf seemed far removed from the Classics, and I thought that such an answer would be deemed frivolous and be the subject of ridicule. So I made the instant craven decision to say nothing – a decision which for me has been the subject of shame and regret for the well over 60 years since. After a silence from the rest of the hash, the Uncle sighed and exclaimed: "Oh my dear sirs, he is the Golf Correspondent of *The Times*. I used to read his articles in *The Times* long before I started to play golf".

The other great golf writer of the 20th century was Henry Longhurst, although his equally compelling style of writing was quite different to Darwin's. Longhurst was at school at Charterhouse and so is featured in this book. It is wrong however to assume that what Darwin and Longhurst wrote in later reminiscences, as opposed to their contemporaneous reports, is always accurate. In the Author's notes on page 156, I draw attention to a number of factual errors relating to Old Carthusian golfers made by both of them.

During Bernard Darwin's time at *The Times*, there were to be found in the sports pages extensive reports about amateur golf in general and the Halford Hewitt Tournament in particular. These have been invaluable sources for me. However after Darwin's retirement in 1953, such reports, although carried on for a time by his successor Peter Ryde (a Carthusian, incidentally) and others, gradually decreased and have now long since disappeared altogether. The British press has decided that amateur sport of any kind is no longer of any interest. To the despair of many of its readers, *The Times* has slavishly followed suit. As regards golf, one searches (usually in vain) for even the results, let alone any report, of the Walker Cup, the Amateur Championship and Amateur International matches; and nowadays the Halford Hewitt is virtually ignored. 50 years ago, anyone interested in golf would have been well aware that Michael Bonallack was the current Amateur Champion. Hands up anyone who knows the name of the current Amateur Champion – or indeed any Amateur Champion in the last ten years.

But enough of this senile wittering. A preface is the place where an author can express his gratitude for all the help he has received in compiling a book of this kind, and I wish to take full advantage of the opportunity. The current President of OCGS, Roddy Gamble, and a supporting Sub-Committee not only entrusted me with the preparation of this book, but have allowed me free rein to get on with it, with much encouragement but without interference. Many others have provided me with information and photographic and other material, but I hope I will be forgiven for mentioning particularly (in alphabetical order), Simon Barrow, Linda Bayman, Mark Benka, Martin Christmas, John Gill, Peter Goodliffe, Julian Hill, Michael Langford, Nick Moore, Barnaby Mote, Graham Pratt, Iain Quick and Dickie Gilbert Scott. In addition, Catherine Smith of Charterhouse Archives has dealt with my numerous requests for information and help with patience and diligence.

I am especially grateful to Catherine Hollingworth, who is responsible for the design of this book. The result of her admirable work is plain for all to see, and without her expert professional help, guidance and advice, this book would probably not have seen the light of day.

Finally, I must mention my wife, who for several years now has had to suffer her dining-room being completely taken over and strewn with piles of papers, files, books, photographs and other items which her untidy other half has managed to accumulate. She too will have much cause to celebrate the OCGS Centenary and the completion of this book.

Nigel Hague
January 2012

Foundation of the Old Carthusian Golfing Society

A modern view of the fourth green and the Clubhouse of Worplesdon Golf Club. The first recorded proposal to form an Old Carthusian Golfing Society was made at the club in 1911, and the first Meeting of the newly-formed OCGS was held there in 1912. Worplesdon GC is now the 'home' venue for many of the matches played by the School's golf teams.

Charterhouse holds the distinction of having the Public School Old Boys Golfing Society with the greatest number of wins in both the Halford Hewitt and the Grafton Morrish Tournaments. Although the Society is not the oldest, it was one of the earliest, for the 'Old Carthusian Golfing Society' was founded in early 1912. This is a descriptive but rather unwieldy title, which will be shortened to 'OCGS' throughout the remainder of this book - with nods of acknowledgement and apology to the Old Boys of the Halford Hewitt schools Canford, Cheltenham, Chigwell, Clifton, Cranleigh, and City of London (and doubtless many other schools as well), and also Highgate, whose Old Cholmeleians Golfing Society was founded as long ago as 1905. No apology is offered to the Oxford and Cambridge Golfing Society, which eschews 'OCGS' and abbreviates itself simply to 'The Society'.

However, well before 1912 there had already been informal gatherings of Old Carthusians for golf matches. *The Carthusian* (the 'in-house' Charterhouse magazine) records the results of several matches played earlier between Old Carthusians and 'Brooke Hall', which is the Charterhouse term for the teaching staff at the School.

The first general invitation to Old Carthusians to play in a golf meeting occurred in 1911. Edwin Cawston, a former Captain of the Cricket XI in 1884, invited all members of the Old Carthusian Football and Cricket Club (now the Old Carthusian Club) to a handicap competition to be held at Worplesdon Golf Club. He presented the Cawston Challenge Cup as the main prize, and this Cup is now the handicap trophy competed for at OCGS Spring Meetings. Cawston thus has a strong claim to have been the main founder of OCGS. *The Carthusian* reported that 30 players attended the meeting, which was held on the 23rd October 1911, that the winner was W W Bruce with a score of 79 – 2 = 77, and that 'a Committee had been formed for the purpose of instituting an Old Carthusian Golfing Society'. This Committee became the founders of OCGS.

Cecil Woodbridge (1886–1951), one of the founders of OCGS, who was in the 1884 Cricket XI captained by Edwin Cawston. He was Captain of Sunningdale GC in 1911.

The first OCGS Minute Book, in an entry which is undated but which records a meeting in the early Spring of 1912, states that eight Old Carthusians had met on more than one occasion and had decided to form a Golfing Society which Old Carthusians would be invited to join. The stated intention was that the Society should hold two meetings a year and play matches against other societies and clubs. That intention has stood up well to the passage of time, and basically remains the same today.

Why 'Carthusians'?

When Thomas Sutton founded Charterhouse as a school and a hospital in 1611, an area with buildings near Smithfield in London which had previously been used as a Carthusian monastery was purchased for the site of his foundation. Carthusian monks were members of an austere monastic order. The boys at the new school were dubbed 'Carthusians', and after a little time this name was adopted officially. The name survived the removal of the School from Charterhouse in London to its present site at Godalming in 1872. Boys (and now girls) at the School are known as Carthusians, and so become Old Carthusians when they leave.

Edwin Cawston (1866–1920), as Captain of the 1884 Cricket XI *(seated centre, holding cricket bat)*, who can claim to be the main founder of OCGS and who was its first Hon Treasurer. He presented the Cawston Challenge Cup, which is the handicap trophy at the Society's Spring Meetings. The *Charterhouse Register* records that he also 'introduced ostrich-farming to America'. Others in the photograph are *(standing second left)* C M Woodbridge, a founder-member of OCGS and *(seated right)* Charles Wreford-Brown, a former Captain of OCGS mentioned below.

The eight founders were, in alphabetical order: W W Bruce; E Cawston; E Garnett; Capt J Harvey; G O Smith; J L F Vogel; C M Woodbridge; and O E Wreford-Brown. Of these, G O Smith is featured below, and Wreford-Brown was a member of an extensive Carthusian family, also featured below. The eight founders were good representatives of Charterhouse sport, for most of them had been considerable games-players at school. Cawston, Smith, Garnett and Wreford-Brown had each been Captain of the Cricket XI,

Woodbridge had also been in the Cricket XI and Smith, Vogel and Wreford-Brown had been in the Football XI. Cawston and Garnett had both been in the Rackets pair. In addition, Bruce and Harvey were both good golfers, and each of them won the scratch prize at early OCGS meetings. Woodbridge was the first Hon Treasurer of Sunningdale GC and had recently been Captain of that Club, and his relative Cyril was for many years a member of the Charterhouse Halford Hewitt side and the Hon Secretary and Treasurer of OCGS.

The eight founders constituted themselves a Committee, and drew up some Rules. They appointed Lord Alverstone, then the Lord Chief Justice, as the first President, and Prince Albert of Schleswig-Holstein, featured below, as the first Captain. The founders also appointed Vogel, one of their number, as the first Hon Secretary, and he duly sent out invitations to Old Carthusians to join the new OCGS.

Lord Alverstone, the first President of OCGS.

Lord Alverstone, previously Sir Richard Webster, had been an outstanding athlete in his youth, and had become an enthusiastic golfer in later life. He was also a cricketer and had been President of the MCC in 1903. He would probably have proved to be an ideal President of OCGS. But early in 1912 he retired from being Lord Chief Justice on the grounds of ill-health, and it appears that on the same grounds he soon resigned the office of President of OCGS. A few months later, the Committee appointed Rev G S Davies, then the Master of Charterhouse in London, as President, and he held that office until his death in 1927. He had formerly been a housemaster at the School at the time of its removal from London to Godalming, Surrey, in 1872. The boys' houses at Charterhouse are mostly named after the housemaster at that date, and hence the house 'Daviesites'.

Rev GS Davies President of OCGS 1912–27. A painting by FH Round, formerly a 'drawing master' at the School.

However, Rev Davies seems to have been a figurehead President, taking little or no interest in the affairs of the Society. At a Committee Meeting after his death, the Captain Halford Hewitt rather pointedly suggested that his replacement should 'be a golfer who would take some interest in the affairs of the Society'.

The Wreford-Brown family

O E (Oswald) Wreford-Brown (1877–1916), one of the eight founders of OCGS, had played football for England in an amateur international match, as well as for the Old Carthusians in two Arthur Dunn Cup finals. He was the youngest of six brothers, one of whom died very young, with the other five constituting a notable Carthusian family. But in 1916 Oswald sadly died of wounds received in the Battle of the Somme, aged 36. The fifth brother, Claude (1876–1915), who had fought in the Boer War and been awarded the DSO, had previously been killed in the First World War at Ypres.

OE (Oswald) Wreford-Brown, a founder of OCGS, who lost his life in the Battle of the Somme in the First World War.

Major William Wreford-Brown, cartooned by Charles Ambrose in 1911. He was then Secretary of Worplesdon GC.

The eldest brother of the family, Major William Wreford-Brown (1865–1941), became the first Secretary of the newly-founded Worplesdon Golf Club in 1907. Despite his age (he was then about 50 years old), he rejoined the Army during the First World War to serve as a staff officer, and did not return as Secretary after 1918. Worplesdon was the venue of the initial meeting of Old Carthusian golfers in 1911 mentioned above and of the first meeting of the newly formed OCGS in 1912, and is the golf club where the senior Charterhouse golf teams now play their 'home' matches.

The second brother, Charles Wreford-Brown (1866–1951), achieved great distinction as a footballer, playing for the Corinthians and England with G O Smith and succeeding him as Captain of the full England XI. He also played for England in several amateur international matches, and later became a senior figure in the Football Association. In 1936 he was the manager of the England Football XI at the Berlin Olympics, and caused something of a sensation by refusing

Tony Wreford-Brown (1912–1997), a member of four winning Arthur Dunn Cup teams, two of them whilst a master at Charterhouse. He became a Housemaster and was also Master in charge of football and later Master in charge of golf.

to allow his team to give the Nazi salute. As well as also being a Gloucestershire county cricketer, and a golfer who was Captain of OCGS in 1924–5, he was a noted chess player.

Charles Wreford-Brown had three sons. The second son, Peter Wreford-Brown, was for many years the Hon Secretary of OCGS and is featured on p.118. The third son, A J (Tony) Wreford-Brown, became the Master in charge of football and a Housemaster at the School, and also latterly the Master in charge of golf. Not surprisingly, they were both in the Football XI, Tony becoming Captain of both the Football and the Cricket XIs.

The third brother Gerald (1874–1956) was also in the Football XI, and became a clergyman. He was a member of OCGS.

Charles Wreford-Brown, formerly England football captain, who was Captain of OCGS in 1924–5.

Halford Hewitt, who is featured at pp.93–96, photographed in 1930, when he was almost 60 years of age. Although not one of the original founders of OCGS, 'Hal' (as he was generally known) had competed in OCGS meetings and other golfing events prior to the First World War, playing off a low single-figure handicap. He became a leading figure in OCGS and was the President of the Public Schools' Golfing Society from its foundation in 1924 until his death in 1949.

First Meetings

The first golfing meeting of the newly formed OCGS took place at Worplesdon GC on Friday 12th July 1912, and the first General Meeting was held on the same day. The competitions included a handicap competition for the Cawston Challenge presented by the Hon Treasurer and a House Challenge Cup presented by the Wreford-Brown family. The General Meeting recorded its thanks to the donors. It was also reported to the Meeting that 134 members had joined OCGS in response to the Hon Secretary's letter to Old Carthusians.

The next golfing event of the new OCGS was an Autumn Meeting held in October 1912 at Walton Heath GC which attracted 40 competitors. Spring Meetings were held in 1913 at Stoke Poges and in 1914 at Oxhey, and there was an Autumn Meeting in 1913 at Sunningdale. There was in addition a foursomes Summer Meeting at Worplesdon in May 1914, at which the OCGS Captain, Prince Albert of Schleswig-Holstein, and Halford Hewitt, who was to become a prominent figure in the Society's affairs and in those of the Public Schools' Golfing Society, were partners and tied for the lead, but lost on a count-back. The Committee had decided that the Autumn Meeting that year should be held at the unlikely venue of Skegness 'or failing that a course in North London'. But the outbreak of the First World War in August 1914 meant that no such Meeting was held, and, like so much else, the activities of OCGS came to an abrupt halt and were not resumed for several years.

The first OCGS Minute Book

Much of this account of OCGS up to the 1939–45 War, particularly the early history, is derived from the Society's first Minute Book. This was carefully written up by successive Hon Secretaries. The Honorary Secretary from 1929 to 1947 was Cyril Woodbridge, a partner in a family firm of Solicitors with offices in the City of London. Those offices were destroyed by enemy bombing in 1941. But Woodbridge's Minutes of the first post-War Committee Meeting held at the East India Club in November 1946 record:

'The Hon Secretary produced all the records of the Society and reported with some satisfaction that he had succeeded in saving the same from the strongroom of his office in Serjeant's Inn EC4 immediately after the complete destruction of those offices in the great blitz of May 10th 1941'.

So the first Minute Book, covering the first 35 or so years of the Society's existence, fortunately survives thanks to the durability of Woodbridge & Co's strongroom. However, there is a long gap in the Minutes between 1914 and 1923. The early years of this period are explained by the First World War, but the absence of Minutes during the later years is puzzling, particularly as OCGS resumed holding both Spring and Autumn Meetings from 1920 onwards.

Unhappily, the other records, including the competition winners and scores at Meetings, meticulously kept and reported by Woodbridge's successor as Hon Secretary, Owen Evans, as being 'intact and complete', have (without the help of enemy bombs) now simply vanished and cannot be traced.

Cyril Woodbridge, Hon Secretary of OCGS from 1929 to 1947, a Solicitor and a member of Royal Mid-Surrey GC, as seen by 'Mel' in 1934. Woodbridge's foresight in keeping the Society's Minutes and record books in his family firm's strongroom avoided their destruction in an enemy air attack in 1941.

G O Smith 1872–1943

After leaving Charterhouse, where he played in the Football XI for three years, G O Smith played football for Oxford University, the Corinthians and England. He became one of the greatest centre-forwards in the history of the game, and the best-known footballer of his day. Between 1893 and 1901, a period when only three international matches were played each season, he played 21 times for England, mostly as the amateur captain of a largely professional team. A nationally known sportsman, he shared with Dr W G Grace the distinction of being known to the public by his initials only (pronounced 'Geo' or 'Jo').

After graduating from Oxford, G O Smith joined the staff of Ludgrove preparatory school, which had been founded by Arthur Dunn, a well-known Etonian footballer. Arthur Dunn died relatively young in 1902, and the Arthur Dunn Cup, the football trophy competed for by old boys of Public Schools, was founded in his memory. On Arthur Dunn's death, G O Smith took over as joint headmaster of Ludgrove at the age of 30. He thereupon retired from international football, but he did play in the first three finals of the Arthur Dunn Cup. In the first year, the Cup was shared by the Old Carthusians after draws in both the final and a replay, but was won by them in the next two years. Smith retired from Ludgrove after the First World War.

Smith also played cricket for Charterhouse for four years, being Captain of the XI for the last two, and for Oxford University. In the 1896 University match, he scored a match-winning fourth-innings 132, and Sir Pelham Warner later wrote that 'as long as there is a history of Oxford and Cambridge cricket the name of G O Smith will be emblazoned on its rolls'.

Little is known of his skill as a golfer, but it seems likely that he played off a low handicap.

Prince Albert of Schleswig-Holstein 1869–1931

Prince Albert of Schleswig-Holstein was one of Queen Victoria's 40 grandchildren, being the younger son of her third daughter Princess Helena who was married to Prince Christian of Schleswig-Holstein. Prince Christian had served with the Prussian Army before the marriage. Prince Albert was educated at Charterhouse, and was in the Cricket XI in 1888. His elder brother, another Prince Christian, was educated at Wellington and had joined the British Army, but died in South Africa whilst serving in the Boer War. As a member of the Royal Family who had died for his country, he attained the status of a national hero, and there is a memorial statue of him at the foot of Windsor Castle. Prince Albert, however, followed in his father's footsteps and joined the Prussian Army, a decision which was understandable and uncontroversial at the time, but which had unhappy consequences.

Prince Albert nevertheless spent a good deal of his time in England, mainly at the family home, Cumberland Lodge in Windsor Great Park. He became an enthusiastic golfer and joined a number of golf clubs, including Sunningdale. In January 1907, he and his sister (another Victoria, and a keen golfer who became President of the Ladies Golf Union in 1914) played in an exhibition match with the 5-times Open champion J H Taylor; and a newspaper report of the match said that 'of late Prince Albert has practised golf assiduously...and has developed into a very sound player' and that 'his form...was estimated by a well-known golfer to be about 9 handicap form'.

At the age of 40, Prince Albert retired from the Prussian Army and returned to live in England. In 1910, he was elected Captain of Sunningdale GC (following his fellow Old Carthusian C M Woodbridge), and in 1912 was elected as the first Captain of OCGS.

He also maintained his interest in cricket. In 1911, he organised and played in a match at Cumberland Lodge between 'Prince Albert's Veterans XI' and Charterhouse. His XI included Dr W G Grace (then aged 63) and other former England Test cricketers. The Charterhouse side was captained by J S F Morrison and included his younger brother R G Morrison, both subsequently Halford Hewitt golfers.

At the outbreak of the 1914–18 War, Prince Albert, who was on the Reserve List of the Prussian Army, felt obliged to return to Germany. He resigned from all his British positions. By a special dispensation from his cousin the Kaiser, he was excused from any service which might involve him in action against British forces. Unsurprisingly in view of the strong anti-German mood of the country at the time, but in sharp contrast to his brother Christian, he incurred a good deal of odium and was sometimes referred

Prince Albert of Schleswig-Holstein, a grandson of Queen Victoria and the first Captain of OCGS.

to as 'the Traitor Prince'. Questions were asked about him in the House of Commons. Having been Chairman of the Old Carthusian Football and Cricket Club (the forerunner of the Old Carthusian Club) in 1911, he had automatically remained an ex-officio member of the Committee of that Club. Some protests were received objecting to this, but the Committee wisely decided to take no action on the matter.

At Sunningdale, suggestions that he should be expelled from membership were discreetly ignored by the Committee. But some members of the Club who had been on active service were disappointed to find that 'the name of an alien Prince is still on the board of Captains'. In July 1918 the Committee took the unusual decision to repaint the Captains' Board, omitting all mention of the year 1910 and the Captain for that year, and that was done. However, in 1927 a motion to restore the year 1910 (and so Prince Albert's name) to the Captains' Board was carried at an AGM by a large majority, and so Prince Albert's name duly appears on the Captains' Board today.

Prince Albert did not return from Germany after the War, and severed all his British connections and ceased to be a member of OCGS.

Horace Hutchinson 1859–1932

H G Hutchinson, christened Horatio but always called Horace, was one of the foremost players in the early years of golf in England. He was a Carthusian, but had only a short time at Charterhouse. The grandson of a former Headmaster Rev J Russell, he entered the School in September 1872, immediately after the School had moved from London to Godalming. But because of ill-health he left at the end of the school year, and so spent only three 'quarters' (the Charterhouse word for school terms) at the School. Hutchinson then attended a local school close to his parents' home near the Royal North Devon links at Westward Ho! This was then one of only a handful of golf courses in England, and was where Hutchinson learned his golf. He won the Club Championship at the age of 15. This caused some difficulty, because until then the winner of the championship had become the Club Captain for the following year.

J H Taylor, later to win the Open Championship five times, worked as a boy for the Hutchinson family, and sometimes caddied for Horace.

Horace Hutchinson was in the final of the first Amateur Championship held in 1885, and won the Championship in both the next two years. He again reached the final in 1903. He figured prominently in many other events, including the Open Championship, and played for England in the first six Amateur International matches started in 1902. In 1887, he published the first-ever golf instruction book, *Hints on Golf*, and thereafter became a prolific writer of books and magazine articles on golf and on many other subjects. He was the author of *Golf* in the Badminton Library series, and his writings contributed to the rapidly spreading popularity of golf. He was also a highly respected golf administrator, and in 1908 was elected the first non-Royal English Captain of the Royal & Ancient.

It is not known whether Hutchinson was ever a member of OCGS (the records have not survived), but it seems unlikely. In 1912, the year of the Society's foundation, Hutchinson suffered a severe illness and underwent a major operation, after which he was tragically unable to play golf or even to walk sufficiently to watch golf.

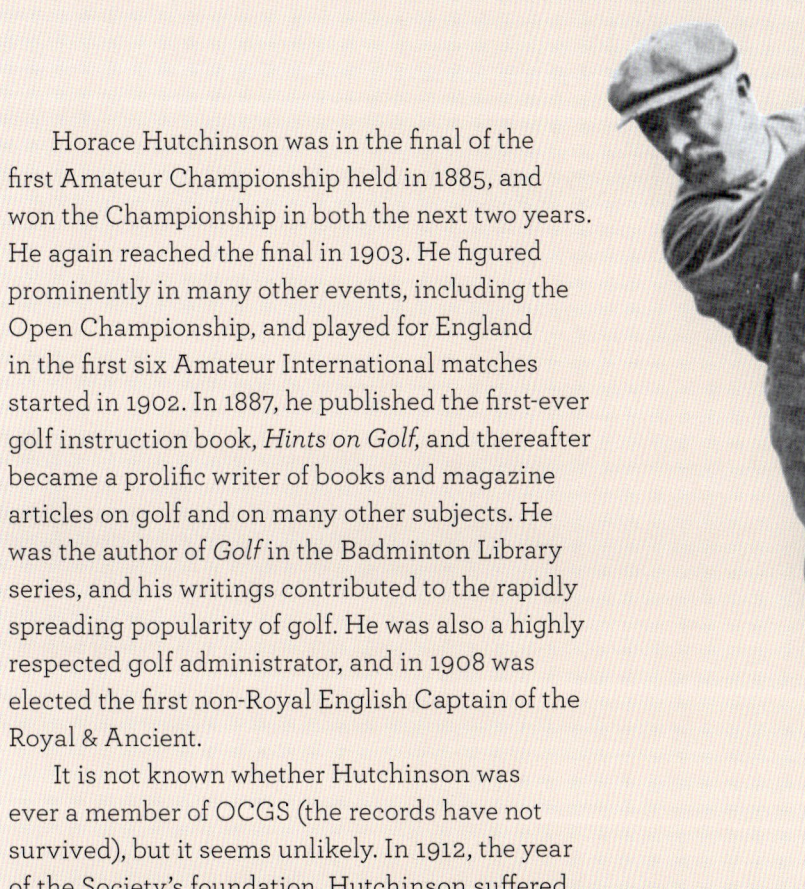

Opposite Horace Hutchinson playing at the 5th hole at New Zealand GC, Byfleet, in an exhibition match in 1899 against S Mure Fergusson (in the other red jacket), finalist in the Amateur Championship in 1894 and 1898. This painting was based on an original black-and-white line drawing used by the Life Association of Scotland, which had sponsored the match, as the centrepiece of its 1900 advertisement calendar. This drawing was later coloured in by an unknown artist, so it is quite possible that the players did not in fact wear red jackets and that the spectators, all insurance company and other officials identified in an accompanying 'Key', were not all attired in dark suits.

The same line drawing forms the basis of a large painting at New Zealand Golf Club. This was commissioned by the Club relatively recently from a Chinese artist, using completely different colours copied from a painting of a similar exhibition match involving Mure Fergusson at Royal St George's GC, Sandwich, which hangs on the wall of the dining-room of that Club. New Zealand GC's painting has been reproduced in *Corinthian Spirit*, Bob Noble's recently published book on Carthusian Sport.

The Halford Hewitt (1)
origins, first tournament, development & captains

The 'Halford Hewitt' (or simply 'the Hewitt') occupies a special place in the hearts of many golfers, and for some it is their favourite golfing occasion of the year. It is a knock-out scratch foursomes Tournament between teams of five pairs representing Public School Old Boys Golfing Societies, and is now played over four consecutive days in the Spring. However, the first 'Hewitt' in 1924 was played over several weekends in 36-hole matches at different courses in the London area. But in the following year the Tournament was played in 18-hole matches over consecutive days at Royal Cinque Ports GC, Deal. This format has stayed unchanged, and Deal has remained the spiritual home of the Tournament ever since. There are nowadays 64 schools which compete, and the Tournament finishes on a Sunday, with the two semi-finals in the morning and the final in the afternoon.

In order to ensure an overall team result, every match has to be won or lost, by playing an extra hole or holes if necessary. In practice, however, once the result of the team match is determined by one team scoring three or more wins, there is little purpose in the other pairs finishing their matches, and the contestants often agree to call their match a half. The record books show many matches as having been halved, but a more accurate result might be 'unfinished'. The rule of playing each match to a conclusion can give rise to odd consequences. For instance, in their 1981 final against Watson's, Charterhouse won two of the matches within 18 holes, but lost one of the remaining three at the 19th hole and the other two at the 20th. So Charterhouse lost 2–3, but if (as permitted in the Grafton Morrish) the matches had terminated at the 18th, Charterhouse would have won 3½–1½.

Neither the players nor the pairings in one round have to be kept the same in following rounds. It frequently happens that, for a variety of reasons, other players are brought in or the pairings changed. So in any year, more than the minimum of 10 players may represent a school. This means that, as nowadays 64 schools compete, at the very least 640 players are involved, which reputedly makes the Halford Hewitt the Tournament with the largest number of players in the world.

How the Halford Hewitt started

There are a number of versions of the origins of the Tournament and the circumstances in which the Carthusian Halford Hewitt, featured at pp.93–96, came to present his Cup. Many of the leading amateur golfers in the early 1920s were well aware of the Arthur Dunn Cup, the football competition between Old Boys of Public Schools started in 1902. Some indeed had themselves competed in the Arthur Dunn, including G L Mellin (a Malvernian for some unknown reason always known as 'Susie' Mellin), a semi-finalist in the 1920 Amateur Championship. The idea of a golf tournament on similar lines naturally occurred to several, including Mellin. From various accounts, including that given by Bernard Drew, a friend and contemporary of all those concerned (and whose word can usually be relied upon), it seems reasonably clear that Mellin mentioned the idea to Halford Hewitt. From that point on, the versions differ.

Bernard Drew, as seen by the cartoonist HH Harris in 1934. Drew played for Charterhouse in their first Halford Hewitt match in 1924 and in several later years, and became both Captain and President of OCGS.

There are however two little-known contemporaneous documents which shed a good deal of light on the matter. The first of these is contained in the Minutes of a General Meeting of OCGS at Walton Heath GC following the Society's Spring Meeting held there on 19th April 1923. The Chairman of the Meeting was Halford Hewitt himself, a prominent member of the Society, and the Hon Secretary was A N (Alexander) Howard.

It is worth setting out the relevant extract in full:

> The Secretary then informed the Meeting that Mr H W Hewitt had been good enough to say that he would offer a cup to be played for by the Public Schools in a Matchplay Tournament. The question before the Meeting was whether in their opinion such a Tournament could be arranged, and the best means of getting it started. At the present time only Eton, Malvern and Uppingham had Golfing Societies. [This was in fact incorrect, because the Uppingham golfing society was not founded until 1925; but others already existed.]
>
> The Chairman said that personally he was only too delighted to foster the game at the Public Schools, and he also said that he did not think it would be very difficult to arrange.
>
> The question was raised how to formulate the Challenge, and it was decided that the committee should arrange the necessary details and the Cup should be played for on similar lines to the Arthur Dunn Cup.
>
> The opinion of the Meeting was then sounded as to whether the match should take the form of 'Foursomes' only, or 'Foursomes and Singles'. The opinion being somewhat divided, a vote was taken on the question which showed that the majority were in favour of 'Foursomes' only being played.

It is to be noted that it seems to have been assumed that each match would be played over 36 holes. The question was whether these should be 36-hole foursomes matches, or whether there should be 18-hole foursomes matches in the morning and 18-hole singles matches in the afternoon (at the time the usual format for fixtures between golfing societies).

The next contemporaneous document is a report in *The Times* of 12th December 1923, giving details of a meeting held 'to discuss conditions of play' for Halford Hewitt's Cup. Only six Old Boys' Societies were represented. No names of individuals were given, but those present almost certainly included Halford Hewitt himself and A N Howard on behalf of Charterhouse and Susie Mellin on behalf of Malvern. The report states:

> It was decided that the competition should be played by foursomes over 36 holes, each Society being represented by five couples. The competition will be begun during April 1924 and the preliminary rounds will be played between given dates on courses to be mutually agreed by the societies concerned… All entries must be sent to Mr A N Howard, hon secretary of the Old Carthusian Golfing Society.

The most familiar, and certainly the most colourful, version of the origins of the Halford Hewitt is that the idea was dreamt up at a convivial lunch at The Addington Golf Club in the summer of 1923. Among those present were the Carthusian John Beck (featured at pp.102–3) and Susie Mellin. Beck and Mellin are said to have to have agreed to inaugurate the Tournament, to have determined that it should be played by foursomes and to have arranged all the other details of the Tournament. So, continues the story, Beck had just commented that all that remained was to find 'some bloody fool' to give a trophy, at which point Halford Hewitt happened to enter the room and was immediately pounced on and persuaded to present a Cup.

It is always 'a pity to let the facts get in the way of a good story', but this version varies completely from the Minute and *The Times* report set out above, and indeed is simply impossible to reconcile with them. Not only is the date of The Addington lunch after that of the Minute, but it is plain that all the arrangements for the Tournament were decided at the Meeting of the 12th December 1923. They had clearly *not* been all decided beforehand by Beck and Mellin or by anybody else. Moreover, Bernard Drew in his (admittedly brief) account of the origins of the Tournament, makes no mention of the story.

In addition, it has sometimes been claimed that Susie Mellin not only founded the Tournament, but organised it from the start. Mellin became the first Hon Secretary of the Public Schools' Golfing Society when it was formed after the first Hewitt had been played in 1924 and did indeed organise the Tournament for many years subsequently. But it is clear that the *first* Hewitt was organised by A N Howard as Hon Secretary of OCGS. Later in the year, after the first Hewitt had been completed, he resigned from that office when he went abroad, and disappeared from the Halford Hewitt scene.

Halford Hewitt was thus the main instigator (or at any rate one of the main instigators) of the Tournament, and played a significant role in its initial organisation. It is unjustified, and unfair to his memory, to trivialise his contribution and characterise him as a mere 'bit-part player', as has sometimes been done. Despite its appearance in a chapter of Henry Longhurst's *My Life and Soft Times* (which hosts several other inaccuracies, as mentioned in the Author's notes on p.156), the suggestion that Halford Hewitt's role was confined to being persuaded to present the Cup does not bear proper examination.

The Halford Hewitt Challenge Cup, together with individual medals for the members of the winning team, ready for presentation to the Captain of the winning school, in the Halford Hewitt corner of a lounge at Royal Cinque Ports GC, Deal. The Challenge Cup is an exact replica (apart from the engraving) of the Cup awarded to the scratch winner at the OCGS Spring Meeting, presented by Halford Hewitt in 1913.

1924 – The first Halford Hewitt Tournament

It was generally thought that the winners of the first Tournament would be either Charterhouse or Eton, but they were drawn against each other in the first round, so that, as Bernard Darwin wrote in *The Times*, 'Fate had unkindly brought together the two strongest teams at first blush'. The match took place at Stoke Poges (now Stoke Park) GC, and was played by five foursome matches over 36 holes. On paper, the Charterhouse side certainly seemed a formidable one. John Beck was unavailable, but the side was to be led by the Walker Cup player Chubby Hooman. It also included Percy Humphreys, who in 1914 had reached the semi-final of the Amateur Championship, and his brother Gerald who had captained Cambridge; John Morrison and Dale Bourn, two other Cambridge Blues, both destined to be England Internationals and stalwart members of seven winning Halford Hewitt teams; and Francis Pegler who had a good record in the Amateur Championship, including a comfortable win in 1921 over Roger Wethered (who tied for the Open Championship later the same year and won the Amateur Championship in 1923).

But things worked out badly. First, Hooman fell ill and was unable to play. His last-minute substitute, Col A E Williams, had formerly been a good golfer, but he was by now well into his 50s and had not played competitive golf for some years. So it was no surprise that he and his partner Alfie 'Baishe' Bower (featured below) lost their match. Secondly, the Humphreys brothers, after journeying up from Stourbridge on the previous day, decided to savour the night-life of London. But matters got out of hand, and they arrived at Stoke Poges on the morning of the match having had only an hour's sleep, and, according to some reports, still in their evening regalia. They were 9 down at lunch time, having lost the first 8 holes of

Victor Longstaffe, as seen at Aldeburgh GC by the cartoonist Mel in 1933. Longstaffe played for Charterhouse in their first Halford Hewitt match in 1924 and on several occasions in the following 10 years. He was OCGS Captain 1947–1949 and President 1949–1954. Contrary to the cartoon, he had not previously been OCGS Captain, but he had been Captain of Stoke Poges GC (as well as of Aldeburgh) and was twice Suffolk county champion.

their match, and were reported to have 'been almost everywhere except in the middle of the course'. Next, Pegler was, according to Bernard Darwin, one of his Etonian opponents, 'much out of practice'; and his partner Victor Longstaffe, a fine golfer who is credited with having founded The Moles GS, could not stave off defeat. In addition, Morrison and Bourn had a distinctly off-day, and were soundly beaten. That left only Bernard Drew, then the Captain of Stoke Poges GC and later to become the long-serving Secretary of Royal Cinque Ports GC, Deal, and Ernest Le Bas as the only Charterhouse winners. Eton duly went on to be the first winners of the Halford Hewitt.

How the Tournament developed

Following the first Tournament in 1924, the Public Schools' Golfing Society was founded in September 1924, with Susie Mellin as the first Hon Secretary. Halford Hewitt was the first Chairman and he remained in that office until his death 25 years later.

The format of five foursomes matches proved popular and successful, and has survived to this day. But the playing of the Tournament over several weekends at a variety of golf courses, adopted from football's Arthur Dunn Cup (in which intervals between matches are unavoidable), proved unsatisfactory. It involved, it was said, too much telephoning and keeping weekends free, and the long intervals between matches tended to make people lose interest. At a meeting in September 1924, it was decided to play the Tournament by matches of 18 holes only, over a few consecutive days, and at a single golf course. Royal Cinque Ports GC, Deal, was chosen, largely at the instigation of Halford Hewitt, a leading member and subsequently the Captain of that Club. Deal has remained the home of the Halford Hewitt ever since.

In 1925, the number of schools competing was only 15 (of whom three scratched), so only four rounds were required and it was easy to complete the Tournament within three days. But the Tournament proved very popular, and more and more schools

A G Bower 1895–1970

Alfie Bower, always known as 'Baishe', was the last amateur footballer to captain England in a full International Football match. This was against Wales in 1925 in the last of his five full international appearances. A full back, he also won 13 amateur international caps. Surprisingly, he had been unable to get into the Charterhouse Football XI, but after leaving school he developed into a first class tall, strong and skilful full back. He played several matches for Chelsea, but played mainly for the amateur Corinthians side, frequently being partnered at back by his fellow Carthusian John Morrison (featured at pp.100–1). Between 1923 and 1930, Bower played in a total of 16 FA Cup matches for Corinthians. In early 1924, he and Morrison were members of the Corinthians side which defeated the then mighty Blackburn Rovers in the first round of the FA Cup, before losing in the second round to West Bromwich Albion after he had been injured early in the match (no substitutes were then allowed).

Later in the same year, both Bower and Morrison played in the first Halford Hewitt match. This was Baishe Bower's only appearance in the Hewitt, although he was selected as a reserve in a number of later years. However his elder brother T C Bower played 11 matches for Charterhouse, and was a member of both the sides which reached the final in 1928 and 1929.

AG ('Baishe') Bower, the last amateur captain of a full international England Football XI, shaking hands with the Belgian captain before the match against Belgium at The Hawthorns, West Bromwich, in December 1924. Earlier in the year, he had played golf for Charterhouse in their first Halford Hewitt match.

The Clubhouse of Royal Cinque Ports GC, Deal, the main venue of the Halford Hewitt since the second Tournament in 1925.

entered each year. By 1932, their number had risen to 35, which meant that six rounds had to be played, albeit with very few in the first round. With only one golf course used, it was no longer possible to finish the Tournament in three days and for several years the final was played on the Monday morning (and followed by a suitably convivial lunch). By 1950, the number of schools wishing to play had risen to 54. There was not enough daylight for all matches to be played on one golf course, and from that date onwards half of the first and second round matches have been played at Royal St George's GC, Sandwich. For practical reasons, it is not possible for there to be more than six rounds, so the number of schools is limited to the maximum of 64, although that number was not reached until 1958.

The Halford Hewitt has shown remarkable resilience. The Tournament was not played during the 1939–45 War, and was not resumed afterwards until 1947. Otherwise, it has been played every year. There were 15 pre-War Tournaments, and up to and including the year 2011, there have since been further 65, making a total of 80. For many years the maximum permitted number of 64 schools have competed.

In the 80 Tournaments up to the end of the year 2011, Charterhouse hold the proud record of having won 16 times, more than any other school. Charterhouse have also reached the final on a further 9 occasions, and have been losing semi-finalists in a further 7 years. As will be seen, in the 2010 final, Charterhouse had what appeared to be an unassailable lead in the final, only for a substantial advantage in the decisive match to slip away and the match to be lost.

Up to the end of 2011, 92 Carthusian golfers had played in the Halford Hewitt, and the individual record of each of them is set out in Appendix 1. Charterhouse have been involved in 1,395 rounds of the Tournament, so playing 6,975 individual matches. It would be impractical, as well as insufferably tedious, to try to summarise the Charterhouse performance in each of those rounds. What follows on pages 33 *et seq* is therefore a summary of the more interesting highlights of the Hewitt over the years.

Halford Hewitt Captains

Initially, the selection of the Halford Hewitt team was made each year by the full Committee, and a captain appointed from the team solely to decide the pairings and make other arrangements during the Tournament. But this cumbersome process proved to be unsatisfactory, and in 1932 it was decided to delegate the selection to an appointed Halford Hewitt Captain and a nominated Sub-Committee. After some years, the nomination of a Sub-Committee ceased, and the Halford Hewitt Captain was authorised to form his own Sub-Committee. The practice nowadays is not to have a formal Sub-Committee at all, but for the Committee to appoint the Halford Hewitt Captain for the year, and leave it to him alone to make his own team selection, although he naturally consults and takes the advice of others.

In addition, the Halford Hewitt Captain is responsible for the selection of teams for the trial matches which take place before the Tournament each year, and also for the general organisation of those matches. He is also usually largely responsible for arranging the accommodation and the social events which then take place, for both the team and supporters.

The responsibility of the Halford Hewitt Captain is therefore a heavy and onerous one. He does not have to be a playing member of the team, and there have been several non-playing Captains. A list of those who have undertaken this task is to be found in Appendix 3.

Jock Moss, non-playing QE Captain 1974, receives the Queen Elizabeth Coronation trophy from RM Saunders the Captain of the Royal Burgess Golfing Society. Moss was also the non-playing Halford Hewitt Captain in 1973 and 1974, and was the first such Captain who had never played in the Tournament. A member of the winning Arthur Dunn Cup football XI in 1936, he became an enthusiastic golfer, and was a frequent and dedicated supporter at tournaments and fixtures involving OCGS.

Moss was Captain of OCGS 1966–69 and President 1979–86. He also served for many years on the Governing Body of the School, and was an influential figure in the founding of the Halford Hewitt golf course there (see pp.133 *et seq*).

The Halford Hewitt (2)
1925–29: a quiet start

During the years up to 1930, OCGS was usually able to field what on paper seemed a strong side, and many good judges fancied Halford Hewitt's Carthusians to win his Cup for him. The side was often headed by one or both of the Walker Cup players Chubby Hooman and John Beck, and contained several other fine golfers. But somehow things did not quite go right, and it was not until 1930 that the Cup was won.

1925

At the beginning of 1925, the Committee of OCGS picked a pool of 17 players from whom the final 10 would be selected. For some unexplained reason, two players not in the original pool, C F Bull and A Ladenburg (in their only appearances in the Tournament), formed the fifth Charterhouse pair. They duly played their part in a surprisingly comfortable 5–0 win over a formidable Winchester side in the first round. In the next round against Malvern, they found themselves in the deciding match. With the score 2–2, they had the better of most of the 18th hole and seemingly had the match won. But, wrote Bernard Darwin in *The Times*, they 'approached the home green too palpably on the instalment system, and let slip their chance'. They also missed a short putt to win on the 20th, and 'the unrelenting Nemesis which never forgets lost chances destroyed them at the next, where they took altogether too maritime a line to the hole' (the English Channel was then much nearer to the 3rd hole).

1926–29

In 1926, in a relatively small field of only 18 schools' golfing societies and with the aid of a bye and a walk-over, Charterhouse reached the semi-final for the first time, but were well beaten by the eventual winners Eton. The following year brought little success, but in 1928 Charterhouse reached the final for the first time. They were lucky to do so. In the semi-final against Cheltenham, the score was 2–2 and the outcome depended on the Charterhouse fifth pair, the experienced Bernard Drew and Eric Prain, then a Cambridge undergraduate, fresh from his first University match. The match looked as good as over when they were two down and Drew topped his tee-shot at the long 16th hole, with the Cheltonians having hit two fine shots to the foot of the bank just below the green. The Carthusians, after what was described as a 'series of adventures', contrived to arrive on the edge of the green after 4 shots, whereupon Drew atoned for his tee-shot by holing a very long putt to snatch an improbable half in 5. They also won the last two holes and the 19th as well. Drew and Prain were again involved in the decisive match in the final against Eton, but this time there was no reprieve.

Bernard Drew and Eric Prain setting off in the first final of the Halford Hewitt contested by Charterhouse in 1928. Drew was an experienced golfer who had played in all four previous Halford Hewitt teams, but Prain was then aged 19. Drew and Prain had won the deciding match at the 19th hole in the Charterhouse semi-final 3–2 win against Cheltenham, but lost the pictured match by 2 & 1. It was the deciding match in the final which was lost to Eton 2–3.

1929 saw the second losing final. Having scraped through the semi-final against Uppingham by winning the decisive match at the 20th, Charterhouse lost 1–4 in the first of four finals contested against Harrow. Halford Hewitt himself was there and, wrote Bernard Darwin, 'praying with averted eyes over every Charterhouse putt. Prayer, however, will not avail against the stronger side and Harrow were the stronger'.

EM (Eric) Prain (1908–1998) was a regular member of the winning Charterhouse Halford Hewitt sides in the 1930s, and also played in five years after the 1939–45 War. In 1946, he published an eloquent and witty little gem of a golf instruction book with the descriptive title *Live Hands*, a neat summary of the author's main theme. Over 45 years later, *Live Hands* was 'discovered' by Wally Armstrong, then a leading US teaching professional, and Tom Lehman, the American winner of the 1993 Open Championship, and in 1994 they re-published it in the USA. They were sensible enough to leave the original text, including an Introduction by Bernard Darwin and some dated black-and-white photographs, completely unaltered, adding only their own prefaces and some occasional comments.

Prain was an exact contemporary of Henry Longhurst, both at Charterhouse and Clare College, Cambridge, and they were in the same Cambridge golf teams. Prain was the Cambridge Captain in 1930 and also played in the following year under Longhurst's captaincy. Prain became a journalist, reporting on many subjects (including golf), and also a newspaper leader-writer. In later life he also became a skilled artist, and several of his paintings were exhibited at the Royal Academy.

The Halford Hewitt (3)
1930–1939: years of triumph

Derek Drayson, a member (and Hon Secretary) of the 1932 Cambridge University golf team. A subsequent loss of hair and the disappearance of a youthful slim waistline resulted in him acquiring in golfing circles the affectionate nickname of 'the Monk'. See photo p.144.

Throughout the 1930s, Charterhouse were undoubtedly the dominant force in the Halford Hewitt. They won the Tournament in seven of the ten years, reached the semi-final in another year, and only lost narrowly by the odd match in the remaining two years.

Several factors accounted for this dominance. The first, and most important, was that the Old Carthusians had a wealth of excellent golfers to choose from. It was often said that the Charterhouse reserve side would beat most other schools. Several fine golfers, such as George Adams, Ken Braddon, and Alan Snelling (to mention only a few) found themselves as reserves, and playing only occasionally. So too did stalwart veterans of many previous Hewitt matches, such as Victor Longstaffe, Cyril Woodbridge and Bernard Drew. Derek Drayson, a Cambridge Blue in 1931 and 1932 and a pre-War member of the OCGS Committee, did not play until 1948, following which he was involved in 46 matches, winning well over half of them.

Secondly, the selectors resisted the temptation not to disturb successful teams, and frequently introduced new players, even into winning sides. Moreover, the new players were not all young golfers fresh from University such as Henry Longhurst, Cecil Middleton and Pat White, who would all continue to form the backbone of the Charterhouse side until well after the 1939–45 War. Lionel Burden-Sanderson and Gerry Weare were both aged 35 when they first played in 1930 and 1933 respectively, and Jack Thompson was in his late 20s when in 1930 he played the first of his 74 matches in

33 years. Weare and Thompson also both continued as post-War stalwarts. To illustrate the changing composition of the Charterhouse side, it is interesting that of the winning 1930 side, only half its members were still in the winning 1939 side (John Beck, Dale Bourn, Lionel Burden-Sanderson, John Morrison and Jack Thompson).

Thirdly, it was generally acknowledged that the Charterhouse sides were essentially team players. It was known that there was discord in some school sides, in that A insisted on playing with B, and C would refuse to partner D. By contrast, the Carthusians cheerfully accepted whoever was allotted to them, and cared only for the success of the team – an admirable tradition which happily has continued to this day.

Finally, Charterhouse teams in this era greatly influenced the character of the Tournament. As Donald Steel, several times a Fettesian opponent, wrote in *Country Life* many years later: 'They dominated the 1930s with a cheerful confidence and were largely responsible for the more or less accepted tradition that, however seriously the golf is taken, it is not the only thing that matters at Deal'.

Victor Longstaffe, OCGS Captain 1947–1949 & President 1949–1954, with 'Tip' his regular caddie at Aldeburgh GC.

1930

1930 was the year of the first Charterhouse win. Despite the fact that Charterhouse had reached the final in both the two previous years, the selectors that year brought in new players. One was Lionel Burden-Sanderson, who for several years formed a successful partnership with John Beck. He was a keen big-game hunter and, it was rumoured, used to dash off to Africa immediately the Tournament had finished, abandoning his clubs in the left luggage office at Victoria Station until the next year. Another was Jack Thompson, then a farmer in South Lincolnshire and a member of Hunstanton GC, who subsequently moved south and joined Rye GC. He was twice the Norfolk county champion, and had a well-deserved reputation as a particularly good iron player.

The Charterhouse win was a popular one. Bernard Darwin in *The Times* wrote: 'Everyone was truly delighted that the donor of the cup, which has given so much pleasure to other people, should at last have the supreme pleasure of seeing his old school win. To see him, when it was all over, wreathed in smiles and flanked by the Morrisons, was alone worth the visit to Deal'. But the win did not come easily. Early rounds against Eton and Harrow were won only 3–2, with the decisive match hole being won only at the 18th hole in each case; and two of the matches in the 4–1 win in the final against Uppingham were similarly won only at the 18th.

1931–33

Charterhouse as the holders came down with a bump the following year. The side scraped home against Westminster in the first round, despite a heavy defeat for the formidable top pair John Beck and Eric Prain who were 'sent to the dogs and the vultures'. Beck and Prain made amends by winning 7 & 6 in the next round, but the side lost to Eton.

1932 however saw the second Charterhouse win with one of the most successful Halford Hewitt campaigns of all time. For the most part, the opposition were simply swept aside. During the whole Tournament, Charterhouse lost only one of the 20 matches in the four rounds played, winning the final against Rugby 3–1, with one match unfinished. The second round match against Eton, however, was much closer than final 4½–½ result suggested. At one point Eton were well up in two matches and also 1 up on the 17th tee in the top match against the two Walker Cup players Chubby Hooman and John Beck. But Hooman and Beck won both the final holes to scrape home by a hole, Jack Thompson and Victor Longstaffe won on the 18th after being 4 down with 8 to play, and Gerry Weare and Cyril Woodbridge came back from 3 down to halve their match.

Gerry Weare, as seen by cartoonist Mel, at the Nevill GC, Tunbridge Wells, 1934.

G. M. ADAMS
Handicap 1.
Old Oxford
Golf Blue.

George Adams (1906–1994) was a member of the winning Charterhouse Halford Hewitt sides in 1933 and 1937, and was a regular reserve and team supporter in other years. He was also Captain of OCGS from 1970 to 1972. He is remembered for an incident following the Oxford v Cambridge match played at Prince's, Sandwich, in 1928. Oxford had lost, and George himself had lost his 36-hole singles match. Following the after-match dinner at the Guilford Hotel (now demolished) on the Sandwich Bay Estate, he decided that a good way to help forget these disasters would be to take a ride on top of the hotel's lift. When the lift stopped at the floor below, he somehow managed to prise open the lift gates, and stepped onto its roof. But being made of only thin plywood, the roof was unable to bear his weight, and George crashed down into the lift-cage itself.

In 1933 Charterhouse warmed up for their defence of the Halford Hewitt by playing a 12-a-side foursomes match at The Addington GC against a formidable team of professionals arranged by Halford Hewitt himself (as *The Times* put it, 'under the aegis of the presiding genius of Deal'). The professional team included three former Open Champions (James Braid, Sandy Herd and J H Taylor), two future Open Champions (Alf Perry in 1935 and Alf Padgham in 1936), as well as four other Ryder Cup players (W H Jolly, A J Lacey, Fred Robson and CA Whitcombe). Perhaps not surprisingly by, the professionals lost only two of the 12 matches, halved one and won the remainder, mostly by comfortable margins. In the Tournament itself, Charterhouse reached the semi-final. Beck and Burden-Sanderson won the top match against Harrow, but although most of the other matches went down the 18th, Charterhouse lost them all and so Harrow won 4–1.

Pat White, a schoolmaster at Harrow, who was a regular member of the Charterhouse Halford Hewitt side from 1933 to 1956.

In the 1933 Oxford v Cambridge match at Prince's, Sandwich, White played a celebrated 36-holes singles match against his Charterhouse contemporary Cecil Middleton. Bernard Darwin considered that the match contained the best combined golf that he had ever seen in the University match ('I have no doubt about it at all'). Both played superbly, with 'one brilliant thrust after another being met by an equally brilliant riposte'. A halved match would have been the only just result, as Darwin, well-known as a rabid Cambridge partisan, acknowledged. Many years later he wrote: 'The Cambridge man had, as I remember, a putt to win. He missed it, and I was glad of it. If I could say more, I would'.

1934–37

There followed four successive years when the Tournament was won. Eton won successive Hewitts in the first three years of the Tournament, but no other school has won four in a row. The most comfortable win was in 1934. This was the first year in which Henry Longhurst, fresh from Cambridge, played and began a long and very successful fifth pair partnership with John Morrison. Charterhouse had a trouble-free passage to the semi-final, where they met Eton once more. This time there were again some close individual matches, but all of them were decided in the Carthusians' favour so a rather flattering 5–0 score was recorded. A close top match in the final against Watson's went to Charterhouse when a topped second at the 18th failed to jump the stream crossing the fairway and 'there was a splash that brought joy to Carthusian hearts'. Three other matches were won comfortably, to the evident joy of Halford Hewitt. *The Times* reported that 'so far as a sore foot would allow him, the pious founder danced a fandango of patriotic delight and the best of all tournaments ended in a blaze of sunshine'.

The 1935 win was much less comfortable, and Charterhouse won only narrowly in four of the six rounds played. Victor Longstaffe played as a substitute in the first round and (wrote Bernard Darwin) 'pretending to be far too old gave his usual faultless exhibition of foursomes play, cheered by the fact that he had at last found somebody whom he could outdrive'. A 3–2 win over Harrow in the second round was secured only when in the deciding match, after Pat White laid a difficult pitch-and run dead at the 17th, he followed it with a wood out of the rough to within a few feet of the hole at the 18th, and so 'took the bread out of the Harrovians' mouths'.

Halford Hewitt dancing 'a fandango of patriotic delight' after Charterhouse had won the 1934 final.

Big game hunter Lionel Burden-Sanderson *left* with John Beck at Deal, partners in the 1934 Halford Hewitt.

The Charterhouse Halford Hewitt Captain for that year was Cyril Woodbridge. In the quarter-final, which was won comfortably, he had played poorly and had lost all confidence, so he took the decision to drop himself from the side for the remaining rounds. Longstaffe once more substituted in the semi-final against Rugby, which was again won by only the slenderest of margins. One win was recorded by White and Cecil Middleton after they had been 3 down, 'White again showing the qualities of a true and tigerish killer by holing a putt on the last two greens'. Morrison and Longhurst also won after being down, and Beck and Burden-Sanderson won only at the 19th. In the final against Shrewsbury, Bernard Drew (taking a respite from his onerous duties as Secretary of Royal Cinque Ports GC) took over from Longstaffe as the substitute, playing his first match in the Tournament after an interval of six years. He and his partner Gerry Weare won their match with some comfort. The score in the final was again 3–2, but this time there was less drama. In the second match, Dale Bourn (wrote Bernard Darwin) 'seemed at times determined to drive into the sea; he failed, but he lost a hole or two in the brave attempt'. Fortunately 'there was a touch of pathos' about the golf of one of their opponents, and so Bourn and Jack Thompson won fairly comfortably. The only close match again involved White and Middleton, who won at the 17th where, after Shrewsbury had narrowly missed their putt, 'White, with a horrid serenity, holed his putt for a 3, and Charterhouse were home again'.

After comfortable wins in the first three rounds of the 1936 Hewitt, Charterhouse had a bad scare against Eton in the fourth. For once, Morrison and Longhurst lost, as did the equally reliable White and Middleton. But Bourn and Thompson delivered a point, as did Eric Prain and Gerry Weare. So all depended on Beck and Burden-Sanderson. All seemed well when they were 3 up, but their lead disappeared, and Beck had to hole an 8ft putt to stay alive at the 18th. In it went, and at the 19th, with Eton over the green and taking 5, Charterhouse had what the Etonian Bernard Darwin

Halford Hewitt *left* at his happiest, presenting his Cup to John Beck, Captain of the winning Charterhouse team in 1936. In the centre background are team members *l to r* Henry Longhurst, Cecil Middleton and Pat White.

generously described as 'a super-gloriously splendid 3' to win the whole match. After that, there was less drama. Charterhouse were always winning both the semi-final against Harrow and the final against Rugby.

The second round of the 1937 Hewitt saw what was described in *The Times* as a 'match of a century'. In the second round against Winchester, the score was 2–2, and everything depended on the match involving Dale Bourn and Cecil Middleton. They had been

Winners of the Halford Hewitt 1936, defeating Rugby 3½–1½ in the final.

Standing JH Thompson   FGC Weare   EM Prain   RL Burden-Sanderson   HC Longhurst

Seated CF Woodbridge *Hon Sec OCGS*   JSF Morrison   Halford Hewitt *Captain OCGS, holding Cup*
JB Beck *HH Captain*   PHF White   CV Middleton

Front Ben Travers 'trainer'   TA Bourn

4 up at one point, but the lead evaporated and they were one down playing the 18th. There Bourn sank a long putt for a birdie 3 to square the match, and followed that by holing a tricky 6-footer for a half at the 19th. The 20th was also halved, and now let the inimitable prose of Bernard Darwin in his *Golf Between Two Wars* (where however he wrongly dates the match) take up the story:

'The Wykehamists played the long third hole with absolute correctness, two good shots and a pitch which ended a few yards straight behind the hole. Not so their adversaries, for Bourn's second went floating away to the right into the country of shingle and the best Middleton could do was to dislodge it into the valley short of the green. Bourn did the right thing, he bumped the ball up out of the valley with some straight-faced iron and let it run to the hole. I see him now racing up to the hill-top and watching the ball pursue its relentless course to end stone-dead. If ever there was a brand snatched from the burning that was it, and somehow after that the end seemed predestined'. (Charterhouse in fact won with a birdie 4 at the 23rd, where Bourn holed yet another putt, converting a fine pitch by Middleton.) 'It was very, very hard on Winchester but they had to yield to the devil that was that day in Dale's jerkin'.

This epic contest was immediately followed by another narrow win, against Tonbridge, but the following rounds including the final were won with relative ease for the fourth win in a row.

1938–39

The third round of the 1938 Tournament at last saw the Charterhouse run of 25 consecutive winning matches come to an end. It was unlucky 13 for Gerry Weare and Eric Prain who had been undefeated in their previous 12 matches together, and their unexpected defeat contributed to the loss to Watson's. Perhaps they missed the inspiration of the presence of Halford Hewitt himself who, because of ill health, had to miss his Tournament for the first time.

But 'Hal' was back the next year, when Charterhouse made amends by winning once more in the looming shadow of the 1939–45 War. They made the most of their opportunity, for as John Morrison wrote in *The Bystander*: 'If Halford Hewitt had made the draw himself, I do not see how he could have done better for his side'. A 3–2 win in the final against Harrow ensured that they became the holders during the next seven years when the Tournament was not played.

The Halford Hewitt (4)
1947–1959: a post-war win & two finals

1947

John Beck

After an eight year gap due to the 1939–45 War, the playing of the Halford Hewitt was resumed in 1947. The Charterhouse side for that year showed surprisingly little change from the winning side of 1939, and 9 of the 11 players who had been involved were re-united. One change was inevitable, for Dale Bourn had lost his life in the War. He was replaced by Ken Braddon, who had been a reserve and occasionally played before the War. However, this remarkable continuity meant that the side was made up of experience without the balance of youth; the youngest member was aged over 35, four (Beck, Snelling, Thompson and Weare) were in their late 40s and John Morrison (the only survivor from the first Hewitt side in 1924) had reached his mid 50s. So Bernard Darwin in *The Times* was justified in referring to them as 'the Old Guard', although after their comfortable first round win he conceded that 'if they creak at all in their venerable joints, it was certainly not perceptive to the eye'.

The following four rounds resulted in narrow wins by the odd match until they reached the final. This turned out to be a repeat of the 1939 final against Harrow (who however fielded only five of their 1939 side). The final was eagerly awaited, but proved to be something of a disappointment. Only Pat White and Alan Snelling were successful for Charterhouse and Harrow had their revenge, winning with some ease.

1948

For a time it seemed certain that Charterhouse would reach the final again in 1948. In the semi-final against Winchester, Cecil Middleton and Peter Needham (then a new recruit playing in his first Hewitt) narrowly won what was thought at the time to be the decisive match, for Longhurst and Braddon had won, and Prain

The 1948 Halford Hewitt team. Peter Needham was playing in his first Hewitt, but all the other members of the team had played in 1939. John Morrison played only in the first round. Charterhouse lost in the semi-final to Winchester, when Eric Prain and Pat White lost at the 24th after being 4 up with 8 to play.

Standing JSF Morrison   HC Longhurst   KV Braddon   AG Snelling   DA Drayson   FGC Weare *reserve*
CF Woodbridge *supporter*   OE Evans *Hon Sec OCGS*

Seated CV Middleton   PHF White   JH Thompson *HH Captain*   JB Beck   EM Prain

Front PWG Needham   Ben Travers *'trainer'*   VCH Longstaffe *Captain OCGS*

and White ('fine golfers and determined killers') were 4 up with 8 to play. But they then suffered a series of disasters and contrived to lose the whole of their lead and be brought back to all square by the 17th. From then on, one half followed another until the 24th where, after a topped second, Winchester managed an unlikely 4 to win the match. As Darwin wrote 'it must be owned that Charterhouse had asked for it by a most unCarthusian collapse'. It would be another 62 years before an even worse 'unCarthusian collapse' would occur.

The winning 1949 Halford Hewitt team, beating Rugby 3–2 in the final. All except Morrison, Travers and Longstaffe played. However, Owen Evans and Cyril Woodbridge both played in the first round only, taking the places of Eric Prain and Cecil Middleton (who had not arrived), but winning their matches. Woodbridge was a veteran of many earlier Hewitts, but it was the only occasion when Evans played.

Standing OE Evans *Hon Sec OCGS*   JSF Morrison *reserve*   CF Woodbridge *Captain OCGS*   KV Braddon   DA Drayson   CV Middleton   PWG Needham   RD Forbes-Watson

Seated PHF White   HC Longhurst   JH Thompson *HH Captain*   JB Beck   EM Prain

Front Ben Travers *'trainer'*   VCH Longstaffe *President OCGS*

1949

'The indomitable Charterhouse have done it again', reported Darwin after their eighth win in the 1949 Hewitt. Prain and White made some amends for their collapse of the previous year by winning four of their five matches together, including an 8 & 6 win with some fine golf against two luckless Wellingtonians in the semi-final, and a win in the final against Rugby when they were 'obviously the better golfers'. Needham and Middleton won two decisive matches by 1 hole in the only two close matches, against Rossall in the fourth round and Rugby in the final, Charterhouse winning both by 3–2 margins. They were not to know, but it would be 17 years before Charterhouse won again, with an entirely different team.

1950–57

In 1950, *The Times* looked forward with eager anticipation to a second round match between Charterhouse as holders and Harrow, thought to be the strongest team. 'Then the guns will flash and swords glitter and there will be no quarter given'. In two of the matches, Charterhouse had easy wins, Gerry Weare and Peter Needham unexpectedly beating a strong Harrovian pair, and Henry Longhurst and Ken Braddon romping home by 6 & 5. But, although two of the other matches went to the 18th green and it 'was a bonny fight', alas the third point would not come.

This was followed by a fallow period. New younger players came in who would form the backbone of the side in future years. Gerald Bristowe was still not yet 18 (and was one of the youngest competitors ever) when he first played in 1952. Dickie Gilbert Scott, Jeffrey Agate and Alan Cox were introduced in 1953 and Michael Bryant in 1954. But despite this

Jeffrey Agate, finalist in the 1954 President's Putter and Halford Hewitt player.

The 1956 Halford Hewitt team, in celebratory mood after defeating two Scottish schools in the early rounds without losing a match. The celebrations may have been excessive. They were certainly short-lived, because the team suffered a whitewash defeat at the hands of the eventual winners Eton in the third round.

Standing AJ Cox   HCD Whinney *supporter*   MW Nesbitt   JOH Greenly   GJ Agate   MC Bryant
RS Gilbert Scott   GR Bristowe   PHF White

Seated OE Evans *Hon Sec OCGS*   Bernard Drew *Sec R Cinque Ports GC and Captain OCGS*
Ben Travers *President OCGS and 'trainer'*   JB Beck   JH Thompson

injection of fresh blood, in the period from 1951 to 58 Charterhouse lost almost as many matches as they won and failed to reach the latter stages of the Tournament. One particularly disappointing year was 1956, when Loretto and Edinburgh Academy were both beaten without losing a match and it looked as if Charterhouse might progress to the final and even regain the Trophy. But, alas, in the third round they crashed out to Eton, losing all five matches, and it was little compensation that Eton were the eventual winners.

Gerry Weare in his 60s and Gerald Bristowe in his early 20s, Halford Hewitt partners in 1957 and 1958. They won seven and halved one of their nine matches together.

1958

Matters improved considerably when Charterhouse reached the final in both 1958 and 1959. By then, only two of the pre-War stalwarts (John Beck and Gerry Weare) remained. Michael Bryant and Alan Cox had established themselves as a reliable fifth pair and had begun to rival Morrison and Longhurst in that role, winning in the two years 11 out of their 12 matches; and their only loss came as a result of one of their 1958 opponents holing at the 18th with what *The Times* described as 'a low scuttling shot from 100 yards out which fell into the hole'. The Charterhouse passage to the 1958 final was fairly comfortable, and the final (once more against Harrow) proved to be a close match. At the end of the 13th hole, Charterhouse were ahead in three matches and all square in another. But then some putts went astray and Harrow just got home 3–2 by winning the top three matches.

1959

The 1959 Tournament saw the first appearance in the Charterhouse side of Martin Christmas, who won five of his six matches, losing only at the 20th in the other. He had an unusual experience at the first hole of his opening match. The opposition, Ampleforth, had arrived with only nine players, but an urgent search unearthed as a substitute a games-playing schoolmaster with a set of golf clubs. Perhaps by way of a sacrifice, he and his partner were, unknown to Christmas and his partner John Beck, pitted against them in the top match. Christmas and Beck were surprised to see one of their opponents wielding a lofted club on the first green. It transpired that the substitute was not only unaware that stymies had been abolished several years previously, but also had not in fact played any golf since the War. Needless to say, Christmas and Beck had a comfortable win. In the same round, although not in the later rounds, Gerry Weare was partnered by his son Ted, one of the few instances of a Hewitt father-and-son partnership, but subsequently emulated in 1993 and 1996 by Carthusians Peter and Mark Benka.

The 1958 Halford Hewitt team, losing finalists by 2–3 to Harrow. Martin Christmas then aged 17 was still at school when the team was selected, but was invited to be present for the experience, and did not play.

Standing DA Drayson   GM Adams *supporter*   JOH Greenly   HC Longhurst *supporter*   PWG Needham   AJ Cox   JC Moss *supporter*   FGC Weare   B Drew *Sec R Cinque Ports GC*   JSF Morrison *supporter*

Seated NC Royds   JB Beck   Ben Travers *OCGS Captain and 'trainer'*   RS Gilbert Scott *HH Captain*   GR Bristowe

Front HCD Whinney *supporter*   MC Bryant   OE Evans *Hon Sec OCGS*   MJ Christmas *supporter and caddie*

The 1959 passage to the final was a difficult one, with three of the matches being won only by the narrowest of margins. In both the fourth round against Rossall and the semi-final against Eton, the outcome depended on the final match which ended all square after 18 holes. But the reliable Alan Cox and Michael Bryant won each time at the 19th. For the semi-final, the Charterhouse side did not include John Beck, then in his 60th year. The Halford Hewitt Captain Dickie Gilbert Scott had taken the sensible decision to rest him, but to play him in the final in place of Gerry Weare, then well into his 60s. But Beck did not take kindly to this decision. At lunchtime, he announced that if he was not good enough to play in the morning he was not good enough to play in the afternoon, and consequently he had not bothered to bring his golf clubs to the course. So Gerry Weare had to play again in the final against Wellington. It mattered not, for he and Martin Christmas cantered through their match, winning 6 & 5.

But the rest of the final was very close. In the top match Dickie Gilbert Scott and Gerald Bristowe played the better long game golf, but their opponents holed putts from everywhere and beat them on the last green. Another pair also lost there, but Cox and Bryant duly won again. So that was two matches all, and everything depended on the fourth pair Derek Drayson and Simon Barrow. They were ahead playing the 17th, and when the Wellingtonian pitch at that hole was hit thin and heading for the cross-bunkers, it seemed that Charterhouse were home. But the ball somehow skipped the bunkers, and Wellington survived. Drayson's hooked drive into thick rough lost the 18th, and three putts at the 19th meant that the chance of victory had been lost.

Dickie Gilbert Scott *left* and Jack Thompson, friends and members of Rye GC, who played in aggregate over 200 Halford Hewitt matches, discuss old times. However their Hewitt careers only overlapped in five years, and they were never partnered together.

The Halford Hewitt (5)
1960–1969: a win & close matches

1960–65

In the first six years of the 1960s, seemingly strong Charterhouse sides won most of their early rounds with some comfort, but failed to reach the final stages of the Tournament. In 1962, they lost narrowly to Stowe in the quarter-final. Charterhouse won the last two matches by wide margins, but although the other three matches were close they were all lost. In 1963, Charterhouse lost another close contest to the eventual winners Fettes, a powerful side which included Donald Steel who would later be the architect of the Halford Hewitt golf course at the School. A repeat match was played in the quarter-final in 1964, but again Fettes won, this time more comfortably, on their way to lifting the Cup in successive years.

1965 saw the first of his 107 appearances for Charterhouse of Peter Benka, featured on p.112. But only Nick Royds and Michael Langford won in the first round against Haileybury. As all the other pairs lost, Charterhouse suffered a first round exit for only the fourth time. It was darkest before dawn.

1966

The dawn saw a comprehensive win in the Tournament, the first for 17 years. Charterhouse had by some margin the best team. The first two pairs (Martin Christmas/Simon Barrow, and Dickie Gilbert Scott/Michael Langford) both won all six of their matches, and out of the total of 30 matches played, only three were lost in the whole Tournament. Moreover, nearly all the wins were comfortable ones, with only one match being won in extra holes. In the same year Charterhouse also won the Grafton Morrish. The successes of the year were duly celebrated by a Luncheon at the Savoy Hotel.

1967–69

A repeat win looked to be on the cards in 1967 after a narrow 3–2 win against Tonbridge in the first round, when Nick Royds and Gerald Bristowe won the decisive match at the 19th. But after a comfortable second round win, the roles were reversed against Eton, the eventual winners, who won 3–2. All the matches were

The 1964 Halford Hewitt team, which reached the quarter-final, but lost to Fettes.

Standing GJ Agate   JC Moss supporter   DB Miller supporter   GM Langford   RS Gilbert Scott   GM Adams supporter   RV Braddon   BTG Nicholson supporter   PWG Needham   DDS Comer   GR Bristowe

Seated JK Shipton Acting Secretary OCGS   NC Royds   OE Evans Captain OCGS   MC Bryant HH Captain   DA Drayson   MJ Christmas

very close, Martin Christmas and Simon Barrow with a 2 & 1 win being the only pair on either side to win before the 18th. Royds and Bristowe were again involved in the decisive match in extra holes, but this time they were defeated.

1968 and 1969 were likewise disappointing, easy wins in the first round being followed by 2–3 defeats in the second.

Richard Braddon, winner of the 1958 Boys Championship, and son of Ken Braddon, former Halford Hewitt player. Richard played in 71 Halford Hewitt matches between 1960 and 1983, and was a member of five winning teams.

The winners of the 1966 Halford Hewitt, defeating Malvern 4–1 in the final.

Standing HCD Whinney *President-elect OCGS* GM Langford SR Barrow DB Miller *supporter* MJ Christmas PJW Benka RV Braddon JC Moss *Captain-elect OCGS* PWG Needham *supporter*

Seated OE Evans *supporter* GR Bristowe PG Wreford-Brown *Hon Sec OCGS* RS Gilbert Scott *HH Captain* DA Drayson *Captain OCGS* NC Royds AJ Cox MC Bryant GJ Agate *supporter*

The Halford Hewitt (6)
1970–1979: two wins

1970–71

After an early round loss in 1970, Charterhouse were winners once more in 1971. The first three rounds were won without the loss of a single match, but the next three were won only by narrow 3–2 margins. In truth, however, it was only the final against Marlborough which was really close. Martin Christmas and John

Winners of the Halford Hewitt 1971, defeating Marlborough 3–2 in the final.

Standing MC Hughesdon   GM Adams *Captain OCGS*   RV Braddon   JR Barnett   SR Barrow   JB Beck *supporter*   GM Langford   JC Moss *supporter*   DB Miller *supporter*   NAC Moore *reserve*

Seated PG Wreford-Brown *Hon Sec OCGS*   PJ W Benka   DA Drayson   MC Bryant *HH Captain*   OE Evans *President OCGS*   RS Gilbert Scott   MJ Christmas

Barnett won in the country, and Michael Bryant and Richard Braddon remained unbeaten for the Tournament by registering a 2 & 1 win. The final two Charterhouse pairs were both beaten, so all depended on the first pair Peter Benka and Dickie Gilbert Scott. A fine birdie 4 at the long 16th put them 1 up, and they managed to hang onto this lead to secure victory.

1972–74

There was only modest success in the two following years. However 1974, 50 years after the first Halford Hewitt, saw another comprehensive Charterhouse win. In the six rounds, only five matches were lost and Donald Steel in *Country Life* wrote that 'it is doubtful whether, even in their best days, they ever won as commandingly as they did this year'. There was, however, only the narrowest of 3–2 wins against Tonbridge in the third round, which was secured only when Alan Cox and Simon Barrow won at the 18th.

1975–79

Charterhouse were defeated in the second round in both 1975 and 1976. In 1977, two wins in extra holes by the first pair Peter Benka and Anthony Royds proved decisive in the third and fourth rounds. But in the semi-final, they were unable to continue the sequence and lost at the 20th, a result which helped Marlborough to gain some revenge (albeit by only a narrow margin) for their 1971 loss in the final.

In 1978, Charterhouse suffered a first round loss to Harrow, the eventual winners. This was one of those matches which would have had a different result if halves had counted. Martin Christmas and Iain Quick had a 6 & 5 win, and Dickie Gilbert Scott and Angus Lloyd also won by comfortable margin. But there was one loss, and both the other two matches were lost in extra holes, one at the 19th and one at the 21st.

After a loss in an early round in 1979, one Committee member commented that the recent record in the Halford Hewitt had been disappointing and urged that there should be trials on a wider basis 'to break the stranglehold that the establishment had on the selection of the side'. However, it was generally felt that this comment had little justification. The following years saw only the usual minor changes in the composition of the side, which was to embark on its most successful period since the halcyon days of the 1930s.

Martin Christmas *left* and Peter Benka, Carthusian Walker Cup players and Halford Hewitt 'centenarians'.

The Halford Hewitt (7)
1980–1989: three wins in a row & a final

After a poor start in 1980, when Repton inflicted a rare first round defeat by the margin of 1–4, Charterhouse had a very successful four-year period in which they followed a final in 1981 with three successive wins. No other school has accomplished this feat since the 1939–45 War. This was the best Charterhouse run since the seven wins in the 1930s. Arguably, it was of comparable merit, for the number of schools then competing was considerably smaller and the competition less strong.

1981

Up to the final in 1981, there was only one close match, Whitgift being defeated only when Anthony Royds and Peter Benka won their match at the 20th. The final against Watson's was a nail-biting affair. Nick Moore and Jeremy Sutherland Pilch in the fourth match and Angus Lloyd and Iain Quick in the fifth match registered solid wins, but the top three matches all went to extra holes. Royds and Benka this time lost at the 19th, and Richard Braddon and Martin Christmas suffered the agony of taking three putts to lose at the 20th. Meanwhile, one of the Watsonian opponents of Michael Hughesdon and Dickie Gilbert Scott, who were comfortably on the 19th green, stole the match by chipping in from off the green. It was another of those contests where, if halved matches counted half a point, Charterhouse would have won 3½–1½. But the result was a 3–2 win for Watson's.

Peter Benka

1982

A virtually unchanged team, under the astute captaincy of Peter Benka, made up for the previous year's disappointment by a convincing win in the Tournament. Only 4 of the 30 matches played were lost. Although two of the losses were in the semi-final against Loretto, Charterhouse won all the other three matches in that round by handsome margins. The score at the end of the final against Dulwich was a seemingly comfortable 4–1, but there were many anxious moments before Dickie Gilbert Scott and Peter Goodliffe won at the 20th and Richard Braddon and Martin Christmas won at the 21st. If both pairs had lost, victory would have gone to Dulwich.

1983

Charterhouse, the holders, notched up another win. They had an easy time of it up to the final, losing only 3 of the 25 matches played up to that point. But the final against Shrewsbury proved to be desperately close. Comfortable wins were exchanged in the fourth and fifth matches. But the first pair, Peter Benka and Michael Hughesdon, having won all of their previous five matches, lost by one hole, a result balanced by a victory for Richard Braddon and Martin Christmas by the same margin in the second match. So all depended on the third match, in which Iain Quick and Richard Bidwell (who had won four of their previous five matches) finally got the better of the Salopian pair only at the 21st.

Roddy Gamble celebrates escaping with a half in the 1984 semi-final, while his partner Nick Moore lifts his cap and shakes hands with their Watsonian opponents.

1984

Once again, Peter Benka captained the Charterhouse side to their third win in the Tournament in successive years. Benka led from the front, and, partnered by Michael Hughesdon, won all his six matches. After a serene passage through the early rounds, the quarter-final match against Radley looked as if it would be close, until Jumbo Royds and Jeremy Sutherland Pilch won at the 19th on their way to five wins in the five matches which they played together. It was they who also clinched the final against Malvern by winning the third Charterhouse point in the bottom match by 2 & 1.

Roddy Gamble, the President of OCGS for its Centenary year, playing in his first Hewitt in 1983, and his partner Nick Moore did not lose a match in that year. In 1984, however, they did not win any of their five matches together, although two of their matches were left unfinished as halves.

David (Jumbo) Royds

1985–86

All good things have to come to an end, and Charterhouse were brought back to earth in the next two years. A narrow 3–2 win in the first round against Bradfield in 1985 was only gained when Peter Benka and Michael Hughesdon won at the 20th, retaining their remarkable record of only one loss in 12 successive matches together. But Charterhouse were beaten in the second round by Watson's. In 1986, Shrewsbury had revenge for their 1983 final loss by winning in the first round. However, the match was very close, because two matches were lost by Charterhouse in extra holes and one at the 18th, with one match left unfinished with an agreed half.

The 1987 Halford Hewitt team, narrowly beaten 2–3 by Tonbridge in the semi-final. Two matches were lost only at the 19th.

Standing CG White reserve   J Sutherland Pilch   RJ Hill   AW Bathurst   DJG Royds   IA Quick   MC Bryant   AJ Wreford-Brown supporter   RW Bidwell

Seated JC Moss former President OCGS   MJ Christmas   RS Gilbert Scott President OCGS and player   JE Bayman Hon Sec OCGS and HH Captain (n/p)   PJW Benka   MC Hughesdon

1987

1987 proved to be another exciting year. After two comfortable wins, the third round opponents were again Watson's. This looked to be a lost cause, but Julian Hill playing in his first Hewitt match and partnered by Andrew Bathurst, from 4 down after 8 holes, won 7 of the next 8 holes with some excellent figures, and Charterhouse were through 3–2. This narrow margin was repeated against the next opponents, Shrewsbury, this time the reliable partnership of Benka and Hughesdon winning the deciding match at the 19th. But the same pair lost at the same hole in the semi-final against

Tonbridge, and the deciding match again went to the 19th, where Hill and Bathurst took three putts to lose. One spectator was Bathurst's father Peter, then the President of the Old Tonbridgean GS, going through the agonies of different emotions arising from his conflicting loyalties.

1988–89

A first round loss in 1988 was followed in 1989 by a third round loss, this time to the old enemy Harrow. Michael Hughesdon and Patric Foley-Brickley battled through to win the top match at the 21st, and Iain Quick and Peter Benka also won. But the other three matches were narrowly lost, two of them on the last green.

Jeremy Sutherland Pilch, who played in the winning Halford Hewitt teams in 1982 and 1984, as well as in the 1981 final. In those three years, he lost only one of his 18 matches. (He was unavailable in 1983.) In 1968 Jeremy won the Belgian Amateur Championship, having been persuaded to enter by Carthusian Derek Goodliffe, who also played in the Championship and who caddied for him in the final. The same Championship has been won in other years by Carthusians John Morrison (1929) and Martin Christmas (1974).

Whilst at Trinity College, Dublin, Jeremy played golf for the University and competed in several Irish amateur events. He experienced at first hand the awe in which the legendary Joe Carr, three times British Amateur Champion and eleven times a Walker Cup player, was regarded in Irish golfing circles. Shortly before he was due to tee off in his match against Carr in a West of Ireland Championship, he was approached by an official who told him that his starting time had been put back 45 minutes 'because Mr Carr wants to watch the Irish Grand National'. Perhaps not surprisingly, Jeremy lost the first two holes of the match, but nevertheless took the great man to the 18th, achieving a much better result than most golfers of the time were able to do.

The Halford Hewitt (8)
1990–1999: a dramatic win

1990–97

After the excitements of the 1980s, the early years of the 1990s were to prove a relatively quiet period. In five of those years (1990, 1991, 1992, 1995 and 1996), Charterhouse won their first two rounds well, but lost in the third round. However in two years 1993 and 1997 only one round was won, while in 1994, Charterhouse suffered their ninth first round defeat. During these years, there were gradual changes to the team with the introduction of new younger players who would form the core of the Charterhouse team in the following years. Mark Benka, the Oxford captain in 1995 started his Hewitt career in 1993, partnering his father Peter in that year and again in 1996.

1998

These changes bore fruit in 1998, when Charterhouse won the Tournament for the 15th time. Thirteen players played in one or more of the six rounds, showing the OCGS strength in depth; and of these, over half had not played before 1992. After two relatively comfortable wins, there was a near squeak against Shrewsbury in the third round on the Friday afternoon. This is reputed to have been the closest of all Halford Hewitt matches, with 96 holes being required to separate the two sides. Richard

Mark Benka, on his way to winning the President's Putter at Rye 2011.

John Bayman, in surgical stockings having recently risen from a sick-bed, with wife Linda, spectators at the 1998 Hewitt final.

Caldwell had fallen ill at lunchtime, and Martin Christmas was called in at the last minute as his substitute. Only Mark Benka and Michael Croft won in 18 holes (and then only by one hole), and Shrewsbury won one match at the same hole and another on the 17th green. But Christmas laid a chip dead at the 21st to win with Michael Hughesdon, and two holeable putts missed by their opposition helped Julian Hill and Simon Stilwell to win at the 22nd and so clinch the narrowest of victories.

The other rounds until the final were won more easily. But the final against a powerful Tonbridge side was full of drama and emotion. When Patric Foley-Brickley and Bill Shipton lost the first 4 holes of their match and were still 4 down at the turn, and two other pairs were also losing their matches, the outlook was far from good. But Mark Benka and Croft kept their 100% record for the year in winning, and Peter Benka and Barnaby Mote had their fifth win in the six matches. Moreover, persistence and patience paid off for Foley-Brickley and Shipton, for they suddenly won five holes in a row in the second half. Tonbridge hit back to square the match at the 18th. So it was down the 19th, with the fate of the Hewitt depending on it. Among the spectators was the gaunt and pale figure of John Bayman, the beloved Hon Secretary, risen from a sick-bed and recovering from his third recent bypass operation. Charterhouse won with a good 4, and the celebrations broke loose. One player recalls leaving the 19th green and looking back to see 'the stooped image of John Bayman and the huge beaming figure of Bill Shipton standing together in tears', adding that 'the sight will live in the memory long after the shine has gone from my Hewitt medal'.

The winning Halford Hewitt team 1998, defeating Tonbridge 3–2 in the final.

Standing l to r RJ Hill PJ Foley-Brickley SJ Stilwell SR Barrow *Hon Secretary OCGS* BP Mote WK Shipton MSP Benka RIC Caldwell MC Croft IA Quick *supporter*

Seated l to r MC Hughesdon PJW Benka GE Pratt *President OCGS* RM Gamble *HH Captain* RS Gilbert Scott *supporter* MJ Christmas.

1999

The 1998 success could not be repeated in 1999, which resembled the early years of the 90s in that the first two rounds were won comfortably enough. (In the first round Julian Hill, partnered by Simon Stilwell, won by a margin of 9 & 8, but later in the year suffered a defeat in the Grafton Morrish by the same score.) However in the third round, Charterhouse again crashed out 0–5, this time to Watson's.

The Halford Hewitt (9)
2000–2011: a win, two finals & two semi-finals

2000–03

The new millennium would bring more success, and Charterhouse re-established themselves as one of the strongest teams. But, like the 1980s, it started badly. In 2000 and 2001, Charterhouse (for the first time in successive years) suffered first round losses, although both were close with the deciding match going into extra holes.

2002–04

Tim Orgill hitting late.

But once again, it proved to have been darkest before dawn, for 2002 saw Charterhouse record their 16th win. Mark Benka and Tim Orgill were paired together for the first time, starting a remarkable partnership in which, usually playing in the top pair against the best players of other schools, they have won over 30 of their 40 matches up to 2011. In the second round against Tonbridge, they closed out a narrow 3–2 win by winning their match at the 19th. 3–2 was also the winning margin in the third round against Dulwich (although the three Charterhouse wins were all comfortable), and Bradfield were beaten by the same margin (but with more difficulty) in the quarter-final. After an easy semi-final win without losing a match, there followed another close match in the final against Whitgift. The top two matches were closely contested, but Whitgift won them both at the 18th and 19th holes. However, the Charterhouse tail wagged, and all the last three matches were won.

The winning Halford Hewitt team 2002, defeating Whitgift 3–2 in the final.

Standing PJW Benka *supporter*   IA Quick *supporter*   RD Tate   SR Barrow *Hon Sec OCGS*   RF Manning
TDL Orgill   NAC Moore *Captain OCGS*   CAM Ayres   BP Mote   RM Gamble *supporter*

Seated RIC Caldwell   SJ Stilwell   PJ Foley-Brickley   MJ Christmas *HH Captain*   RJ Hill   MC Croft   MSP Benka

Another victory in 2003 seemed very probable, for in the five rounds up to the final, Charterhouse swept all before them and only one of the 30 matches was lost. But the final against Edinburgh Academy proved very different. Benka and Orgill kept up their 100% record with a 4 and 3 win (they were not extended beyond the 16th in any round), but this was matched by a Scottish win by the same margin. The other three matches were all close, but Edinburgh just got home in the first two of them to clinch their victory, with the other match left as an agreed half.

The following year, Charterhouse had their revenge for their 2003 defeat in the final with a 3–2 win over Edinburgh Acadamy in the second round, Benka and Orgill winning what proved to be the critical match at the 19th. Another close contest followed in the quarter-final against Merchiston. The score after the top four matches was 2–2, with everything depending on the final match.

Christian Ayres

This finished all square after 18 holes, so Rupert Tate and Christian Ayres had to play extra holes. The first five of these were halved, and the match went on and on. But eventually Tate and Ayres prevailed at the 24th to end one of the longest matches in Halford Hewitt history. However, they were evidently exhausted by their efforts, and lost heavily in the semi-final against Malvern the next morning. Only Richard Caldwell and Patric Foley-Brickley could manage a win, and the match was lost 1½–3½.

2005–09

2005 saw Charterhouse continue their good from for three rounds, only to suffer a 2–3 loss to Rossall in the fourth. 2006 was another of the years where the result would have been different if halves had counted. After wins in the first two rounds, and the score against Watson's at 2–1 to Charterhouse, two matches which were all square after 18 holes went to extra holes, and both were lost at the 19th.

More progress was made in 2007. Charterhouse again reached the semi-final in 2007 with relative comfort, losing only one match in each of the previous four rounds. This brought their number of semi-final appearances up to 32, of which only 7 have been lost. Unfortunately, this was one such occasion, for they were defeated 2–3 by Epsom.

Barnaby Mote

There was an unusual first round encounter with Rugby in 2008, because not a single match went beyond the 14th green. Benka and Orgill won 7 & 6, and Robert Manning and Simon Stilwell won by 5 & 4. But the other three matches were all lost, so Charterhouse suffered another first round defeat. However, the fourth round was reached in 2009. Old foes Marlborough, Whitgift and Wellington were convincingly beaten in the first three rounds. But in the fourth against Merchant Taylors', Manning and Stilwell were beaten at the 19th in the deciding match.

2010

And so to the extraordinary final in 2010, which has to be described in a little detail, painful though it is to a Carthusian. The Charterhouse Hewitt side included players with outstanding scores achieved in winning important events at their Clubs later in the year. Simon Stilwell won at Rye with 66+70=136, Ryan McKinnia at Worplesdon with 68+71=139, and Richard Caldwell at Sunningdale with 68. Moreover, Mark Benka won the King William IV medal at the R & A Autumn Meeting at St Andrews, played in difficult weather conditions, with a remarkable record score of 66, several strokes better than the next best scratch score; and he also won the President's Putter at Rye in January 2011.

Simon Stilwell

So it was not surprising that Charterhouse should figure strongly in the 2010 Hewitt, which had one of the most dramatic finishes in its 80-year history. The early rounds were won comfortably, Charterhouse losing only 2 of the 25 matches played in the five rounds on their way to the final. The other finalists, Clifton, had never won and had only once reached the final, so expectations were high. Moreover, Charterhouse got off to the best of starts. In the first match, Mark Benka and Tim Orgill completed their 6th win in 6 matches with a thumping 6 & 5 victory, and in the second match Simon Stilwell and Richard Caldwell remained unbeaten with a win by the same margin. In addition, when they passed the refreshment hut near the 12th fairway, the Charterhouse third pair Ryan McKinnia and Robert Manning were 5 up with 7 to play, so it seemed to be all over bar the popping of the champagne corks. True it was that the last two matches were close and Clifton, who had adopted the tactic of putting their better players in the later pairs, had a slight edge; but what did that matter?

News of the position was relayed back to Nick Owen, the Hon Secretary of the PSGS, in the Clubhouse. He and others were anxious to complete the presentation of the Cup as early as possible,

Robert Manning

Julian Hill

in order to get home to watch the last round of the US Masters on television. So to save time, he asked the sign-writer to inscribe 'Charterhouse beat Clifton' on the Halford Hewitt Honours Board in the Clubhouse, and then let him depart.

However, anyone who has played golf, particularly foursomes golf, will know from experience how an apparently impregnable lead can easily and quickly melt away. In the third match, Clifton got their 4s at both the 12th and the 13th, and Charterhouse did not, so that was back to 3 up. After a scrappy half in 4 at the long par 3 14th, both sides played the 15th very well, but Clifton holed from off the green for a birdie and Charterhouse just missed; down to 2 up with 3 to play. A Charterhouse victory seemed assured when the Clifton drive at the par 5 16th sailed away towards thick rough, but the ball finished in the open on a sandy track and Clifton scrambled their half in 5 to keep the match alive. Clifton, with the honour at the 17th (playing downwind and with run on the ball), nearly drove into one of the cross-bunkers, some 100 yards from the green and normally well out of range. On the advice of his Halford Hewitt captain, Peter Goodliffe, McKinnia put his metal wood back into the bag and played an iron off the tee for safety. But he struck it beautifully and the ball went on and on until it toppled into one of the cross-bunkers, leaving a very difficult long bunker shot to the green. Manning hit the shot cleanly but the ball cleared the green and finished in a horrid place; so that was down to 1 up. A hook off the 18th tee into severe rough meant the loss of that hole too. The match was now all square, and it would have to go down the 19th.

Meanwhile, in the fourth match Julian Hill and Andy Hollingsworth had recovered from 4 down at the turn to be all square on the 18th tee. The Clifton drive looked as if it was headed for the brook that crosses the 18th fairway, and for a brief moment it appeared that the third pairs would not have to play extra holes. But the ball stopped a matter of inches short of the brook, from where Clifton not only found the green but also holed their putt for a birdie to win the match. Moreover, Clifton had hung on to their lead in the fifth match and won that too.

Old Carthusian Golfing Society 1912–2012

The Honours Board at Deal before the 2010 result had been taped over and subsequently repainted.

Runners-up Halford Hewitt Cup 2010.

Standing MH Faldo *supporter*   AP Hollingsworth   ATH Stanley   Jo Thompson *supporter*   RG McKinnia   TDL Orgill   JS Gill *Hon Sec OCGS*   GE Pratt *supporter*   MHG Boswell *Captain OCGS*   RF Manning   AJB Hill *supporter*

Seated CAM Ayres   BP Mote   MSP Benka   PG Goodliffe *HH Captain*   RJ Hill   SJ Stilwell   RIC Caldwell

So everything now depended on the third match. Charterhouse had much the better of the tee-shots, for Clifton's drive was the shorter by some distance and seemed destined for a bush. But it finished safely in a piece of mown but long grass, hovering a few inches above the ground. Clifton then played an excellent second which found its way onto the green, albeit some yards from the hole. At this critical point, poor Manning, with the fate of empires resting on his shoulders, did what hundreds of other golfers have done and will continue to do; he pitched the Charterhouse second straight into the dreaded stream just short of the green, and that was effectively that. Clifton had come back from the dead and had won against all the odds. And Nick Owen had to tape over the Honours Board for the presentation ceremony and arrange for it to be repainted.

This unexpected downfall of the mighty Charterhouse caused some innocent amusement among other Hewitt players and supporters. One Cliftonian bard was moved to compose a parody of the well-known poem by Sir Henry Newbolt, another Cliftonian, which describes the tense finish of a cricket match at the College with the first line 'There's a breathless hush in the close tonight'. The parody begins:

> *There's a breathless hush on the greens tonight*
> *Five up and seven to play*
> *The sign writer's hand dextrous and light*
> *Poised to make it a Charterhouse day.*

And ends (with unorthodox rhyming):

> *Hapless Carthusians sigh with dismay*
> *As a burn takes their ball a watery way*
> *The spirit of Clifton triumphs again*
> *Play up, play up and play the game!*

Ryan McKinnia

2011

Hopes were high that Charterhouse would be able to put the events of 2010 behind them, and be able to register a win in the last year of the OCGS centenary. But it was not to be. The first three rounds were won, and Benka and Orgill won their match in the fourth round against Malvern, remaining unbeaten for the year. But things went wrong in the final holes of two matches, and the round was lost 1–3, with one match unfinished.

The 2011 Tournament did however bring one consolation. Under 'the Anderson Scales', schools are ranked on the number of team matches won in relation to the number of matches played. For several years, Charterhouse had languished in second place behind Harrow in the Anderson Scale for the whole period of the Tournament (there are other Scales for shorter periods). Although Charterhouse had won more Hewitts, Harrow had been the more consistent. But the five wins in six matches in 2010 had resulted in Charterhouse drawing level to share first place. The three wins in four matches in 2011, enabled Charterhouse to maintain their position as joint leaders in the Anderson Scale and so bring the OCGS Centenary to a happy conclusion.

Peter Goodliffe, Halford Hewitt Captain 2010 and 2011.

The Grafton Morrish

The Grafton Morrish is a tournament inaugurated by Peter Grafton and Peter Morrish in 1963. Their purpose was to enable every Golfing Society of old boys of independent schools to compete. So it differs from the Halford Hewitt by being open to all Golfing Societies of old boys (and girls) of independent schools which are members of the HMC (Headmasters and Headmistresses Conference), and the membership is thus not confined to the maximum 64 contestants allowed in the Hewitt. The Grafton Morrish is a scratch foursomes tournament, like the Hewitt, but with only three pairs per school. The number of schools competing renders it necessary to have regional qualifying rounds, which have now increased to eight in number. These are played in the summer under the Stableford scoring system. 47 schools, together with the previous year's winners (who are now exempt), qualify for the matchplay stages played in September or early October, with 16 schools having a bye into the second round. The Grafton Morrish is played at Hunstanton GC and Royal West Norfolk GC, Brancaster, with the latter stages at Hunstanton.

The Grafton Morrish also differs from the Halford Hewitt in that halved matches are counted as such. Each team is awarded half a point and extra holes are not normally played. But if the result in the other two matches is one all, in order to obtain an overall result the halved match has to play extra holes. In the rare event of both the first two matches also being halved, only the final match goes into extra holes.

All schools competing in the Grafton Morrish are members of the Public Schools Old Boys Golf Association (not to be confused with the Public Schools' Golfing Society). The Tournament has proved increasingly popular. By January 2011, the number of Societies which were members had risen to 159, and has since increased further. The school crest of each of Society is hung on a wall in the Hunstanton clubhouse, with the crest of the holders at the top. Two factors make the Grafton Morrish in some ways a more difficult tournament to win than the Halford Hewitt. The first is the greater competition from the number of schools competing. The second is that strength in depth is less important. Societies with only relatively few good golfers in their number are less disadvantaged. With only six players in a team, the Tournament does not favour the big battalions as much as the Hewitt tends to do.

OCGS did not enter the Tournament in its first two years, but quickly made up for lost time. Under the captaincy of Dickie Gilbert Scott, Charterhouse won in 1965 at the first attempt, defeating Haberdashers' Aske's 3–0 in the final, after defeating on

Dickie Gilbert Scott receives the Grafton Morrish Trophy from Peter Morrish after the first Charterhouse win in 1965. Remarkably, Dickie was a member of the winning Charterhouse team in every one of the eight years when Charterhouse have won the Trophy.

Winners of the Grafton Morrish 1965, defeating Haberdashers' Aske's 3–0 in the final.

Standing PG Wreford-Brown *Hon Sec OCGS*   RV Braddon   PJW Benka   GM Langford

Seated NC Royds   RS Gilbert Scott   MC Bryant

the way two Hewitt schools (Shrewsbury and Sherborne) fairly comfortably, but having closer matches when defeating two other schools (Hymers College and St Peter's, York).

Winners of the Grafton Morrish 1966.

Standing PJ W Benka
TR Murdoch
J Sutherland Pilch

Seated NC Royds
PG Wreford-Brown *Hon Sec OCGS* GM Langford
RS Gilbert Scott

This success was repeated in 1966, completing the double having won the Halford Hewitt earlier in the year. A third successive win was achieved in 1967, when Rydal were defeated in the final. No other school has won the Grafton Morrish three years in a row. These wins have been repeated in five further years (1976, 1978, 1980, 1981 and 1992), and the total of eight wins is three more than any other school.

There were some tense moments in the 1992 win. Unusually, the final stages of the Tournament were played at Brancaster that year, it being the Royal West Norfolk GC's centenary year. With the score against Uppingham in the fourth round at one each, all depended on the match involving Iain Quick and Christian Ayres, whose opponents (aided by a hole in one) were 3 up with 4 to play. But steady Carthusian pars and a fluffed Uppinghamian chip resulted in the match going down the 19th. What was described as 'an anxious stubbed pitch' by Uppingham, and an approach putt by Quick from some distance off the green to the side of the hole, gave Charterhouse a narrow win there. The semi-final against Haileybury was also very close, and it took a birdie at the 18th to enable Charterhouse to reach the final. At this point, Dickie Gilbert Scott, by now aged 68, had played five rounds and done his stuff. He was rested for the final, and (doubtless to the dismay of their opponents Harrow) his replacement was none other than the formidable Peter Benka who had flown in to partner his son Mark. They duly won their match with some comfort, as did the other two pairs.

Winners of the Grafton Morrish 1980, defeating Bolton 2½–½ in the final.
Standing JE Bayman *Hon Sec OCGS* NAC Moore J Sutherland Pilch RW Bidwell DA Drayson *supporter*
Seated RS Gilbert Scott PJW Benka IA Quick JC Moss *President OCGS*

As in the Halford Hewitt, ladies are permitted to play (but off the same tees). In the second round in the following year, two prominent members of the Charterhouse side acquired the unhappy distinction of being the first pair to lose a Grafton Morrish match to a lady. She was a county player, and with her brother, also a county player, they defeated Patric Foley-Brickley and Iain Quick to help Stockport to a 2–1 win. However, there was some balm to the injured pride in the next year, 1994, when Charterhouse again reached the final, losing narrowly to George Heriot's.

Each year the OCGS Committee appoints a Grafton Morrish Captain, who carries the considerable responsibilities of selecting the members of the team for the year and generally organising participation in both the qualifying rounds and the later knock-out stages of the Tournament. In 1982, Iain Quick (who had previously been the winning Captain in 1978) was re-elected Captain for that year, and was subsequently continuously re-elected for over 20 years. According to him, this was done purely on the basis that he 'lived somewhere near' Hunstanton; Carthusians are not strong on their geography of areas to the north and east of London, and the

Winners of the Grafton Morrish 1992, displaying the Trophy, having defeated Merchant Taylors' 2½–½ in the final. Peter Benka played only in the final.

Standing PJ Foley-Brickley CAM Ayres RJ Hill MSP Benka

Seated GE Pratt *Captain OCGS and caddie* IA Quick *playing GM Captain* RS Gilbert Scott PJW Benka

Committee were apparently oblivious to the fact that Iain's home is a difficult cross-country drive of over 100 miles away. But the choice was an inspired and highly successful one. So far as possible, he selected in his teams three young players knocking on the door of Halford Hewitt selection, in order to give them experience of competitive OCGS team golf, and balanced them with three more senior and seasoned golfers. This policy proved both popular and rewarding. 'Quickie' has also been an enthusiastic supporter of the Tournament, and has been the Chairman of the Public School Old Boys Golf Association since 2005.

Iain Quick, Captain of the winning Charterhouse side 1978 (defeating Bolton 2–1 in the final), receives the Grafton Morrish Trophy from Peter Grafton.

Iain Quick, in characteristic golfing attire, as seen by Graham Pratt, formerly President OCGS.

The Queen Elizabeth

Two Scottish golfers, on their train home to Edinburgh after playing in the 1952 Halford Hewitt, discussed the idea of a similar tournament to be held in Scotland. By the time the train pulled into Waverly Station, they had decided to inaugurate such a tournament the following year. That year was to be the year of The Queen's Coronation so, with the appropriate royal consent, they named the tournament 'The Queen Elizabeth Coronation Schools Tournament'. This has been played annually since 1953 at the course of the Royal Burgess Golfing Society (which donated a handsome trophy) at Barnton, Edinburgh. Like the Grafton Morrish, it is a knock-out matchplay tournament between three foursomes pairs from independent schools' Old Boys Golfing Societies.

As might be expected, the majority of entries come from Scottish schools, but English schools are invited. Old Carthusian teams, although often the recipients of good-natured banter, have always been made extremely welcome, in particular at a dinner on the eve of the first round; in recent years Andrew Forgan, for 22 years the Secretary of the Tournament (and now an honorary member of OCGS), has been a particularly helpful and supportive host to the Charterhouse team. The Tournament is held in the Autumn, and although a clash with the Grafton Morrish is always avoided, the closeness in dates of the two tournaments can cause difficulties with the availability of some players. Notwithstanding this, and despite the difficulties and expenses of travel and accommodation (partly met by the Society), OCGS has in most years entered a team.

The 'Queen Elizabeth', as it is generally known, has been twice won by Charterhouse, in 1974 and 2001. Charterhouse also reached the final in 1961, being the first English school to do so, and again in 2010.

Finalists in the 1961 Queen Elizabeth at Barnton.

MJ Christmas   NC Royds
GR Bristowe   MC Bryant
RS Gilbert Scott
DB Miller *QE Captain (n/p)*
RV Braddon

1974

Charterhouse were the first English school to win the Queen Elizabeth, having earlier in the year won the Halford Hewitt. In the final, Royal High School, Edinburgh, were beaten 3–0, but the contest was much closer than the score suggests. The first Charterhouse pair won very easily, but in the second match Richard Braddon holed a very long putt at the 17th to stay all square and then drove to within a few yards of the pin at the

Julian Hill, Captain of the winning 2001 Queen Elizabeth Coronation team, is presented with the Trophy by Mrs Carol Foggo the wife of the Captain of the Royal Burgess Golfing Society, flanked by *left* Michael Croft, Simon Stilwell, Tim Orgill, and *right* Patric Foley-Brickley and Robert Manning.

Robert Manning drinking champagne from the Queen Elizabeth Coronation Trophy after playing a winning shot in the 2001 final, watched by Simon Stilwell *left* and Julian Hill.

short par 4 18th to win one up. The third Charterhouse pair were behind for most of their match, but Peter Benka laid a bunker shot close to the hole to win at the 18th.

2001

27 years were to elapse before Charterhouse were again the winners. But again success did not come easily and there were some dramatic close calls involving all three pairs. With the score at one match each in the first round against Crieff, all depended on the top pair of Simon Stilwell and Michael Croft. Things did not look good when they arrived at the short but dangerous par 4 18th hole one down, but Stilwell holed a difficult 10-footer for a winning birdie, and the 19th was won as well. In the second round against Glasgow Academy, all depended this time on the match involving Julian Hill and Tim Orgill. Again the prospects looked bleak when they were 2 down with 3 to play. But Orgill holed a long putt to win the 16th, and the 17th was also won. At the 18th, Hill hit his drive out of the heel, but was relieved to see it travel straight and low and run onto the green. The opposition succumbed to the pressure and carved their tee-shot out of bounds, so another narrow win from behind was secured.

The next two matches were both won with relative comfort, and in the final against a strong Glasgow High School side, Charterhouse got off to a good start and were 2 up at the turn in all three matches. But the Glasgow HS second pair, who included a Walker Cup player, then had three birdies in a row against Hill and Orgill, and when the match had reached the 16th all square, won the next two holes with a 'gimme' eagle and another birdie. So that was one match down. However, Stilwell and Croft hung on to their lead to complete a perfect tally for the Tournament of 5 wins in 5 matches. So this time it all depended on the bottom match. Patric Foley-Brickley and Robert Manning, who had begun the Tournament with a troublesome back, were more than up to the task, clinching their win with a fine up-and-down from a precarious place in a greenside bunker.

The Bernard Darwin, the Senior Darwin and the Very Senior Darwin

Three Tournaments are played each year at Woking GC involving senior members of those old school golfing societies which were the first 16 original entrants for the Halford Hewitt. The number of schools is limited to 16 to enable knock-out tournaments to be completed in two days, with two rounds on the first day and the semi-finals and the final on the second day. There are other similar tournaments for the subsequent entrants for the Halford Hewitt.

One of the main purposes of the three tournaments is to give the opportunity for Halford Hewitt players to rekindle old rivalries and renew old friendships. However, past participation in the Hewitt is not a qualifying requirement, and the Charterhouse teams frequently include one or more golfers who have never enjoyed the privilege of competing in the Hewitt. For some, the opportunity to represent one's old school is their last remaining sporting ambition.

One such eminent OCGS member who did not play in the Hewitt but has been a member of winning teams in both the Bernard Darwin and the Senior Darwin is Hugh, Lord Griffiths of Govilon, a former Law Lord. A Cambridge Blue at both cricket and golf, Hugh has the rare distinction of having held the offices of both the President of the MCC (1990) and the Captain of the R & A (1993).

Hugh Griffiths
(Lord Griffiths of Govilon)

The Bernard Darwin

This is a four round knock-out competition between teams of three foursomes pairs with a qualification age which was originally 50 but which has now been raised to 55. As in the Hewitt, each match has to be played to a conclusion, with the playing of extra holes if necessary.

An early Bernard Darwin team.
Standing PG Wreford-Brown JH Thompson KV Braddon
Seated OE Evans FGC Weare DA Drayson

Winners of the Bernard Darwin 1975, defeating Harrow 2–1 in the final. Drayson and Miller won the deciding match at the 19th after being 6 down with 7 to play.

Standing AR Gupta   JC Hinman   AJ Cox

Seated DA Drayson   RS Gilbert Scott   PG Wreford-Brown *President OCGS*   DB Miller

Winners of the Bernard Darwin 1998.

IR Woolley   MC Hughesdon   MJ Christmas   RS Gilbert Scott   RM Gamble   GM Langford

'The Darwin' was first played in 1953, and Charterhouse have won it in five years, 1975, 1989, 1997, 1998 and 2004. The most memorable win occurred in 1975 in the final against Harrow. Dickie Gilbert Scott and Alan Cox won their match, but another Charterhouse pair lost, making the score 1–1. In the deciding match, Derek Drayson and Douglas Miller were 6 down with 7 to play, but managed to get back to all square after 18 and then won their match and so the Trophy at the 19th hole.

Winners of the Bernard Darwin 2004.

GM Langford   NAC Moore
PJW Benka   RM Gamble
MJ Christmas
C Spencer-Phillips

The Senior Bernard Darwin

This was first played in 1987, and has the qualifying age of 65. Initially only two pairs per school were involved, and it was decided on the net aggregate of holes up. This exacting form of scoring could lead to some harsh consequences, with every match having to be played out over the full 18 holes, and with the possibility of a substantial win for one pair being overtaken by an even bigger win by the opposition's second pair. Some wins bordered on the

Finalists in the Bernard Darwin 2010.

JPL Davis   NAC Moore
MJC Robinson
JJ Pearmund   RM Gamble
C Spencer-Phillips

embarrassing. On one occasion, the Charterhouse first pair of Dickie Gilbert Scott and Alan Cox inflicted a 13 up defeat on two unfortunates; even a second pair which included the writer could not negate that and prevent Charterhouse from proceeding to the next round. However, more merciful arrangements have now prevailed. The format has now been altered, and the number of pairs per school extended to three, as in the Bernard Darwin itself.

Charterhouse have won the Senior Darwin in four years, 1991, 1994, 2010 and 2011.

The Very Senior Bernard Darwin

This competition (also known as the Almost-Dead Darwin) takes a very different form. The qualifying age is 75, and only one round is played. Each school can enter up to three pairs, who play an individual stableford round with a generously modified par for the course. Most of the long par 4s which the elderly have difficulty in reaching in two are deemed to be par 5s, and the relatively long par 3 2nd hole is deemed to be a par 4. There is no aggregation of scores, and the winners are the pair with the highest number of points. Charterhouse have won in two years, 1992 and 2000.

Some Notable Members

This section contains short biographical sketches of some prominent members of OCGS. The choice of who to include and who to leave out has been the writer's alone, and few will agree with him. But this section is already long enough as it is and, quite apart from the difficulty of selection, it is simply impracticable to include all who merit inclusion. A few others are included in the section on Secretaries. But among those no longer living who have reluctantly been omitted the names of Victor Longstaffe, Gerry Weare, Humphrey Whinney and Jock Moss, each a former Captain and later President, spring to mind, as well as Bernard Drew and several others.

Halford W Hewitt 1870–1949

As a result of his Tournament, Halford Hewitt's name is widely known among amateur golfers, but his unusual first name has sometimes caused confusion. Indeed, some have been under the impression that the Tournament was founded jointly by two persons, as in the case of the Grafton Morrish.

Halford Hewitt's first name was an old family name. His father was Thomas (later Sir Thomas) Hewitt KC, a barrister who specialised in Revenue matters and was the chairman of an insurance company for many years. Thomas Hewitt's father was Halford Wotton Hewitt, a noted antiquarian and citizen of Lichfield. The young Hewitt was given exactly the same names as his grandfather.

'Hal' Hewitt, as he was generally known, became a dedicated and passionate supporter of Charterhouse and all things Carthusian.

"I'd do anything for Charterhouse" he replied to Henry Longhurst's thanks for his hospitality at his house Hardwick Hall, near Bury St Edmunds, over a weekend when an Old Carthusian team played against Royal Worlington GC. Yet it is a surprising fact that Hewitt spent only four 'quarters' (school terms) at Charterhouse. He was a new boy at the age of 12½ but left just after his 14th birthday, and was then educated privately. Why he left Charterhouse so early is a mystery, but the probable reason was ill-health, from which he frequently suffered during his life. It seems unlikely that his parents were dissatisfied with the School, because his younger brother (who rejoiced in the name of Copley de Lisle Hewitt) spent the normal full time at Charterhouse, being in the Football XI for two years and subsequently winning a football Blue at Oxford.

Hewitt went to Clare College, Cambridge, from where he graduated with a degree in law. (The College's archives record his school as 'Private Tuition'.) He then qualified as a barrister, being called to the Bar by the Middle Temple in 1896, but he never went into practice. He did however compete regularly in the annual Bar Golf Tournament, which is open to non-practising barristers, between 1910 and 1931. He played off handicaps between 2 and 5, so (even though comparative handicaps were much lower at the time) in his younger days he had been a rather more competent golfer than is often assumed. He became a familiar figure at Bar Tournaments, but had little success.

After Cambridge, Hewitt went into the City. He became a director of several mining and rubber companies, and had other business interests. However increasing deafness, coupled with frail health, caused him to retire early from his business activities. He appears to have had ample means and leisure, for he spent most of each January at St Moritz enjoying winter sports, particularly curling, in which sport he was frequently the 'skip'. In the 1930s, he presented a Halford Hewitt Cup for ski-ing, to be competed for by Public School teams. Downhill races for the Cup were held at Wengen for a few years, but the event did not attract sufficient support to survive.

Although not a founder member of OCGS, Hewitt was one of the first members and an enthusiastic supporter. Until prevented by ill-health, Hewitt was ever-present at his Tournament, usually going through agonies about the progress of his beloved Charterhouse team, but always presenting his Cup to the winners with grace and good humour.

'Hal' was a popular figure, but treated with affectionate disrespect by Carthusian sides. He became the butt of many practical jokes, and it was said that if he had stretched an inch every time his leg was pulled, he would be the tallest man in England. On one occasion in the late 1930s, by which time Hal had become very deaf, at the lunch after the final of the Hewitt (then played on a Monday morning), John Beck with the connivance of the rest of his audience made an entirely silent 'speech' with glances and gestures towards Hal followed by applause, which the beaming recipient

The elegant gold cigarette case presented to Halford Hewitt in 1933, and its inscription. This is by tradition held by the President of OCGS during his term of office.

'Hal' Hewitt *(standing)* celebrating a Charterhouse victory in 'the Hewitt' with Gerry Weare *left, team member* and Humphrey Whinney *supporter*. Both Weare and Whinney each subsequently became Captain and then President of OCGS.

graciously acknowledged. It was some time before poor Hal realised what was happening.

Hewitt was for many years a leading member of Royal Cinque Ports GC, Deal. He was the Club's Hon Treasurer for many years and twice Captain, in 1929–30 and in 1943–45. He was also Captain of OCGS from 1927 to 1947 and President of OCGS from 1947 until his death in 1949. He was also the first President of the Public Schools' Golfing Society from its formation in 1924 until his death. He was a conscientious holder of all his offices, always making sure that he was present at every committee or other meeting, and sometimes cutting short a holiday or other trip abroad in order to be there.

It has been suggested by some commentators, apparently anxious to belittle Halford Hewitt's contribution to the Tournament which bears his name, that he had always been a golfing 'rabbit' and that when he donated the cup, golf was a new-found hobby. Like the allegation that he did little except accede to a request to donate a Cup (discussed at pp.23–5), these suggestions are, to put it politely, wide of the mark.

Ben Travers 1886–1980

The school theatre at Charterhouse, designed by Dickie Gilbert Scott (see pp.106–8), is named the Ben Travers Theatre. The celebrated dramatist was President of OCGS from 1954 to 1960, and was a greatly loved figure for many Carthusian golfers.

Ben Travers came late to the theatre. After leaving Charterhouse, he worked in the family business for several years, which included a spell in Malaya, and then for a publisher. In 1914, he joined the Royal Naval Air Service, which was subsequently amalgamated with the Royal Flying Corps. He narrowly escaped death when his plane crashed on what is now Brookmans Park golf course, killing the pilot.

After the end of the War, Travers became a writer, and wrote two humorous novels which he turned into farces for the theatre, his real love. The second of these *A Cuckoo in the Nest* was produced at the Aldwych Theatre in 1925 and was a huge success. Travers followed it with several more 'Aldwych farces' (as they became known) in the 1920s and 1930s. Apart from *A Cuckoo in the Nest*, which was revived after the 1939–45 War, his best pre-war plays were probably *Rookery Nook*, *Thark*, and *Banana Ridge*. Travers himself appeared in *Banana Ridge* playing convincingly the cameo part of a Chinese servant with a colloquial Malay accent. After the War, he continued to write plays and film scripts, although with only modest success.

However, in 1975, when he was aged 89, he achieved his greatest theatrical triumph, taking advantage of the relaxation of the Lord Chamberlain's censorship rules, with *The Bed Before Yesterday*. This starred Joan Plowright as a middle-aged woman finding sex for the first time. In an interview on his 90th birthday, Travers was asked whether it was not

Ben Travers in full flow at an OCGS dinner at the Savoy Hotel, using the Halford Hewitt Challenge Cup as a theatrical prop, enjoyed by Dickie Gilbert Scott.

rather late in life to be writing a sex romp and immediately replied that he had an awfully good memory.

Ben Travers was short in stature, but had an abundance of personality, with sparkling eyes and boundless enthusiasm and energy, always cheerful and modest. He was witty, and an excellent after dinner speaker and raconteur, much in demand at OCGS functions. His favourite party piece, which he was often asked to repeat, was his description of the life-style of the fish in the glass tank above some public men's urinals and the consternation caused when the lavatory flushed, told from the point of view of both the onlooker and the fish themselves, complete with facial expressions. Memories differ as to the location of the public urinals; according to Henry Longhurst it was Euston Station, but others say it was Piccadilly Underground or the now demolished Alhambra Theatre, a variety music hall in Leicester Square. It matters not. Anyone fortunate enough to have heard Ben Travers tell his tale is unlikely to forget the experience.

For many years both before and after the 1939–45 War, Ben Travers was an enthusiastic supporter of Charterhouse Halford Hewitt sides, acting as 'trainer', and is to be seen in many of the team photographs. In the mornings, he made sure that the members of the team were properly awake with a supply of Enos salts, and later in the day ensured that they were suitably refreshed with gin, kummel and other supposed aids to golfing excellence.

Although no player, Ben Travers had a love of watching cricket, fostered when he was taken to his first Test Match at the age of seven and saw W G Grace bat. In 1928, he made the long sea voyage to Australia to follow A P F Chapman's England XI on its 1928–29 tour, as a sort of early one-man Barmy Army (doubtless with all the enthusiasm, but hopefully without the excesses, of that fraternity). However after the Third Test Match, when England clinched The Ashes, he was summoned home to attend the premiere of a new Aldwych farce. Following a characteristic and entertaining appearance on radio's Test Match Special when in his 90s, he was persuaded to write a book of cricket reminiscences. These were published posthumously just after his death at the age of 94, under the title *94 Declared*. The book is a very good read.

C V L Hooman 1887–1969

Christened Charles, Hooman was usually known as 'Chubby' Hooman, although photographs of him in his younger days do not suggest that he was overweight. He was the son of T C L Hooman, an outstanding Carthusian all-round sportsman. At Charterhouse, Chubby Hooman played in the Cricket XI for four years, being captain in his final year, 1906. In the same year, he won the Public Schools Noel Bruce rackets championship with R M Garnett. At Oxford, he duly won Blues for cricket and rackets. But golf was the game at which he truly excelled, and he was also a golf Blue in each of his four years.

Hooman is the holder of two unusual distinctions which it is safe to say will never be equalled. First, he is the only man to have played golf in an international match and cricket for the Gentlemen versus the Players in the same year. In 1910, after a successful winter season for Oxford, he was selected to play golf for England v Scotland, and distinguished himself by playing excellent golf to win the deciding singles match. Later in the same year, after an outstanding cricket season for Oxford, he was selected to play for the Gentlemen versus the Players at Lord's. However, by contrast, this was an inglorious failure. Batting at No. 4, he was bowled for 0 in both innings. Hooman played several games for Kent in the same season and helped them to win the County Championship. However, he gave up first class cricket at the end of the year, although he continued to play Minor Counties cricket for Devon.

Hooman's second distinction is that he is the only man to have won a Walker Cup match at an extra hole. Playing in the first ever Walker Cup match in 1922 at the National Links, Long Island, USA, he 'played very, very well' to beat the formidable Jesse Sweetser at the 37th hole. Sweetser was destined to win

Hooman at the crease …

the US Amateur Championship two weeks later ('trampling his way through the strongest part of the draw like some all-conquering Juggernaut', wrote Bernard Darwin) and also the British Amateur in 1926, and to play in a further five Walker Cup matches. Darwin captained the 1922 GB & I side, and let him take up the story:

'Nobody had considered what was to be done in the case of a halved match. When Sweetser and Hooman halved, the two captains, Fownes [the American captain] and I were away in the dim distance; so Fritz Byers, as President of the USGA, sent them off to the 37th, which Hooman won in a sparkling 3. Since then more humane counsels have prevailed and heaven knows that when two men have halved a 36-hole match in the Walker Cup, they have earned an immediate drink with no further demands on them. It was a point which I made clear to Bill Fownes when I was 2 up on the 35th teeing ground'.

Hooman also played in the 1923 Walker Cup, but lost his foursomes match and was not selected for the singles. Thereafter, he seems to have given up competitive golf, and his work and absence abroad often prevented him from being available to play for OCGS in the Halford Hewitt. He did however play in six years (being Captain in two years) and, partnering John Beck, was a member of the winning teams in 1932 and 1937. On his return in 1937 after a long absence, Darwin wrote in *The Times*: 'Here is one of the few golfers with a palpable touch of genius. He emphasised the fact that he was something of a revisiting ghost by using wooden shafts and taking a sand tee instead of your new-fangled pegs'.

... and on the golf course.

J S F Morrison 1892–1961

John Morrison, Captain of the winning Charterhouse Halford Hewitt team,1932. As usual, comfort and warmth took precedence over sartorial elegance.

John Morrison merits a chapter, or even a book, to himself. He played a variety of games at the highest level, all of them for enjoyment. At Charterhouse he was in both the Cricket and Football XIs, captaining both, and then at Cambridge won Blues in both sports. He left Cambridge at the outbreak of the 1914–18 War, and served with great distinction in Royal Naval Air Service and subsequently the RAF, taking part in daring air raids on Otranto. His bravery was recognised by the awards of the DFC and Bar, and it is said that he was recommended for a VC. After the War, he returned to Cambridge, where he captained the football XI and added a golf Blue.

Morrison was one of the leading amateur footballers of has day. A large and strong man, he played full back for the Corinthians (the amateur side which played against the top professional sides of the time) and for the Old Carthusians, forming for both teams a strong full back partnership with his fellow Carthusian A G 'Baishe' Bower (see p.29). He was a member of the Corinthian team which famously defeated Blackburn Rovers, then one of the leading professional sides, in the 1926 FA Cup, and won an international amateur cap in 1920. He also played several games for Sunderland.

As a golfer, Morrison was a law unto himself. A strong big hitter, he used a variety of eccentric golf clubs, some with hickory shafts and some with grips the size of a cricket bat handle. In wet weather he sometimes wore a large waterproof skirt (it was said, in retaliation for women starting to wear trousers) and in the cold wore a teddy-bear coat tied up with string round the middle. Yet his golf improved enough for him in 1930 to add an amateur international golf cap to his football cap. He won the Belgian Amateur Championship in 1929, having won the Worplesdon Mixed Foursomes in 1928, partnered by the great Joyce Wethered. He also partnered her twice to victory in the Sunningdale Foursomes, which, as a Sunningdale member and Captain in 1933, he is credited with founding.

In the Halford Hewitt, Morrison played for Charterhouse in all the 17 years in which the Tournament was played from its inception in 1924 until 1948, a total of 65 matches. He played usually in the fifth pair, in the early years frequently with Victor Longstaffe (they won 10 of their 12 matches together), and from 1934 onwards with Henry Longhurst. Morrison and Longhurst became one of the best known pairs in the Tournament, often appearing over the horizon to confirm that they had duly won the deciding point to clinch another Charterhouse victory. From 1934 to 1939, they lost only 3 of their 31 matches together.

In characteristic pose.

John Morrison, with teddy-bear coat, as cartooned by HH Harris in *The Bystander* 1938.

Morrison was a bluff congenial character, with a prodigious capacity for alcoholic refreshment. When playing football for Sunderland, his captain Charlie Buchan (still a legend at Sunderland) is said to have permitted him by special dispensation to drink a quart of beer before the start of a match and another quart at half-time. Later, among his other tipples, he drank sherry out of a pint mug. John Morrison stories are legion. A favourite one relates to a visit by the Charterhouse Halford Hewitt team to a local pub. "Well, here we are," said Morrison to the barmaid, "ten players and two reserves. We will all buy a round. 144 whiskies, please".

In the 1920s Morrison joined the golf design firm of Colt and Alison, and became a partner in 1930. He was mainly responsible for the design of several good courses on the Continent. In 1937 he also designed a number of new back tees and made alterations to Deal in preparation for the Open Championship which was due to be held there in 1938. The alterations included the completely remodelled short 4th hole which replaced the previous unsatisfactory blind hole known as the Sandy Parlour. But the course suffered severe flooding from the sea in February 1938, and the Championship was switched to Royal St George's, Sandwich. (Similar flooding occurred in 1949, and that year's Open Championship was again switched to Royal St George's.)

Before the 1939–45 War, Morrison was also a golf journalist, writing regular articles for *The Bystander* and other publications. At the outbreak of the War, he immediately rejoined the RAF, and became a Group Captain.

John Morrison had a younger brother, Roggie. Roggie was also a good golfer, and reached the final of the French Amateur Championship in 1930. He was a member of the winning Halford Hewitt side in that year and played again the following year. But although selected subsequently, he was seldom able to travel from his home in south-west France.

J B Beck 1899–1980

John Beck was in both the Cricket and Football XIs at Charterhouse. He left school relatively early in 1917 to enlist in the Army. He served with distinction in the Coldstream Guards and was awarded the MC. After the War, he went up to Oxford where he won a golf Blue. He became a prominent amateur golfer, winning several important trophies such as the *Golf Illustrated* Gold Vase in 1925, the Lord Warden Challenge Cup in 1925 and 1932, the Royal St George's Cup in 1933, the President's Putter in 1937 and the Berkshire Trophy in 1946. He also played in international matches for England, and in the 1928 Walker Cup.

Beck is best remembered for his captaincy of the Great Britain and Ireland side which in 1938 won the Walker Cup for the first time. He had been given the option of playing himself if he wished, but he decided not to do so, and thereby furthered the modern practice of having non-playing captains in golf team events. He was also the non-playing Walker Cup Captain in 1947, although this time without success. Beck was also prominent in golf administration, and was Captain of the R & A in 1956–7. A successful businessman, Beck was a company chairman and for a time was Administrative Director-General BOAC. He became an RAF Group Captain in the 1939–45 War. He was a genial and convivial, if sometimes slightly intimidating, companion, and was an excellent raconteur and after-dinner speaker.

John Beck was much involved in the founding of the Halford Hewitt Tournament, and became a towering figure in Public School golf and OCGS. He was President of OCGS from 1963 to 1966. He was for many years

John Beck, Captain in 1938 of the first GB & I team to win the Walker Cup, receiving the Cup at St Andrews from Col PGM Skene, the deputy Captain of the R & A.

Opposite John Beck sleeps it off.

one of the leading Charterhouse players in the Halford Hewitt, frequently playing in the first pair, and was the winning Halford Hewitt Captain in 1936 and 1937. He played in over 90 Halford Hewitt matches from 1925 to 1963, and but for the War would undoubtedly have been one of the first Halford Hewitt "centenarians". After 1963, he was frequently to be seen at the Hewitt supporting Charterhouse.

Dale Bourn *left* with Jack Thompson at Deal for the Halford Hewitt in 1934. Both were members of the winning Charterhouse side in that year. Thompson played in 74 matches between 1930 and 1963.

T A Bourn 1902–41

'Dale' Bourn, as he was always known (his second name was Arundale) was a half-brother of John and Roggie Morrison. He was in the Cricket XI and the fives pair at Charterhouse, and won golf Blues at Cambridge in 1923 and 1924. From then onwards until the 1939–45 War, he was a well-known amateur golfer, winning the Surrey Amateur Championship in 1927, the French Amateur in 1928, both the President's Putter and the English Amateur in 1930 and reaching the final of the British Amateur Championship in 1933. He was also an English amateur international on several occasions. Bourn was a regular member of the OCGS Halford Hewitt side, playing in every match up to 1939 and thus being a member of the seven winning Charterhouse sides in the 1930s. A mercurial and sometimes wild golfer, he was a fine putter.

Bourn had qualified as a solicitor, but became Personal Assistant to Woolf ('Babe') Barnato, another Old Carthusian, a position which allowed him time to play a good deal of golf. Barnato was the heir to a diamond-mining fortune, and became a motor-racing driver, who as one of 'the Bentley Boys', won many races at Brooklands, as well as the 24-hour Le Mans race in three successive years. Barnato also became the major shareholder of Bentley Motors Ltd, and joined Rolls-Royce when that company took over Bentley Motors Ltd in 1930.

In March 1930, Barnato struck a bet that, driving his Bentley and leaving Cannes station at the same time, he would arrive in London before the express *Le Train Bleu* arrived at Calais. Dale Bourn accompanied Barnato as companion and relief driver. After crossing the Channel by ferry, they arrived at the Conservative Club in St James's Street four minutes before *Le Train Bleu* pulled into Calais station. (However the French police prosecuted Barnato for racing on the highway, and the fine exceeded the amount of his wining bet.) Bourn thus had an eventful first half of 1930, for he also won the President's Putter in January, played in the first Charterhouse win in the Halford Hewitt in April, and both won the English Amateur and played in an international match against Scotland in May.

Bourn joined the Army at the beginning of the 1939-45 War. When serving as a captain in the Royal Artillery, he lost his life in an aeroplane accident in October 1941.

H C Longhurst 1909–78

Henry Longhurst at his home Claydon Windmills, Hassocks, Sussex. Windmills were one of his interests, and he wrote a book on the subject.

After leaving Charterhouse in 1927, Henry Longhurst went up to Clare College, Cambridge. There he seems to have preferred golf to study. Although a Classical Scholar of both Charterhouse and Clare College, he obtained no better than a Third in each part of the Economics Tripos. But he won a golf Blue in each of his four years, captaining the side in his final year.

In 1932, some articles written by Longhurst for a small magazine *Tee Topics* came to the attention of the editor of *The Sunday Times*, who offered him a job as the first golf correspondent of that newspaper. Longhurst's association with *The Sunday Times* lasted over 45 years. In due course, his short articles, nearly always on the back page of the paper, became essential reading for golfers and were also greatly enjoyed by others. He also wrote weekly articles for *The Tatler* and became the golf correspondent of the *Evening Standard*. For many years he contributed articles to *Golf Illustrated*. He also wrote the excellent book *Golf* (1937, re-issued with additions in 1947) in the Modern Games series. Other books written by Longhurst include *It Was Good While It Lasted* (1943), *I Wouldn't Have Missed It* (1945), *Spice of Life* (1963) and *My Life and Soft Times* (1972), all readable and entertaining reminiscences.

However, Longhurst became best known to the general public as a result of television. When the BBC first started televising the Open Championship and other events, Longhurst provided the commentary. His style was to say little, letting the pictures on the screen speak for themselves, but in his dry laconic way was master both of telling the viewer the essential scores and other facts, and of describing for handicap players and non-golfers the emotions of the players caught on camera. His commentary style was particularly popular in the United States, where viewers normally suffered endless chat and a surfeit of superlatives from their commentators.

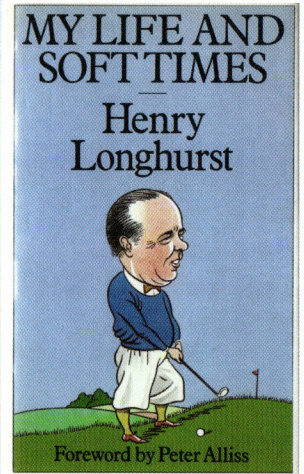

The first edition of the book has a different cover and this cover appears only on later editions.

Longhurst had many other interests. In 1943, he was elected to Parliament as Conservative MP for Acton, supporting the Wartime coalition, but lost his seat in the 1945 Labour landslide.

Longhurst was a good amateur golfer between the Wars, winning the German Amateur Championship in 1936 and reaching the final of the French in 1937. He first played for Charterhouse in the Halford Hewitt in 1934, forming an celebrated partnership with John Morrison as the fifth pair. In the years up to the War, they were beaten in only three of their 31 matches, a formidable record (albeit not quite as good as he later claimed in *My Life and Soft Times*). He also played in a further 25 matches after the War, the last being in 1956. For some years he remained a supporter of OCGS at Deal. He was a good raconteur and excellent company, even if he always expected his glass to be topped up.

R S Gilbert Scott b. 1923

Dickie Gilbert Scott had the unusual experience of attending two Public Schools, having been at Harrow for three years before arriving at Charterhouse in 1940 at the age of 16. After leaving school, he studied at an architectural college and then did military service in the Airborne Division of the Royal Engineers. Thereafter, he qualified as a Chartered Architect and joined his father's firm.

Dickie's first encounter with OCGS came in a telephone call in early 1953 from Owen Evans, then Secretary of OCGS, who asked him whether he was a member of the Old Harrovian Golfing Society. On receiving the answer 'No', Evans then invited him to join OCGS and participate in some Halford Hewitt trials. Dickie accepted, was duly selected for the Charterhouse side that year. So began an extensive and distinguished Halford Hewitt career. Dickie played in every year except one from 1953 to 1992, and was a member of six Cup-winning teams. He played a total of 128 matches, more than any other Carthusian, and is one of only a handful of players who have played in the Halford Hewitt, the Bernard Darwin and the Senior Bernard Darwin Tournaments in the same year. The only year he missed the Hewitt was 1970, after an accident in which he suffered several rib fractures. He was a passenger in a car driven by the Carthusian Peter Ryde, the golf correspondent of *The Times*, ironically returning other Carthusians back from a dinner following the year's Halford Hewitt draw. Dickie was also for many years a prominent member of the OCGS teams which competed in the Grafton Morrish, playing in every one of the eight OCGS teams which have won the Trophy. He was also a regular member of the OCGS team in the Queen Elizabeth.

Dickie had a text-book golf swing, elegant and powerful and with an enviable rhythm, which, allied to an excellent short game and a serene temperament, made him into a formidable player. (The past tense is used because, sadly, a troublesome back now prevents him playing golf.) Although he was considered by many to be among the best amateur golfers in the country, he played in only a very few tournament events, and preferred to reserve his limited time for golf for his friends and for the Old Carthusians. (He did, however, win the Berks, Bucks and Oxon County Championship in 1955.) It was always a surprise if he did not win the scratch prize at the OCGS Spring and Autumn meetings when he competed.

Dickie was an architect of some distinction until his retirement in 1999. Among many projects to his credit are the restoration works and alterations to The Guildhall in the City of London through several phases, including the construction of the Library and the Art Gallery, and a headquarters building for Blue Circle Industries plc

Dickie Gilbert Scott

Displaying faultless technique at the opening of the Halford Hewitt golf course, 1988.

at Aldermaston (constructed from that company's cement products), for both of which he received architectural awards. But for Carthusians, Dickie is best noted for his design for Charterhouse of seven new Houses accommodating 60 boarders each and a Dining Block seating 500 in the 1970s, and also the later construction of the School of Technology, a Music School and the Ben Travers Theatre. As his father, Sir Giles Gilbert Scott, was the architect of the imposing War Memorial Chapel, the landscape of the modern Charterhouse owes much to the Gilbert Scott family. However, the otherwise excellent pictorial history of Charterhouse in the Cloisters at the School fails to make the connection, referring blandly to 'architect Richard Scott'.

J E Bayman 1932–2005

After leaving Charterhouse and completing National Service, John Bayman joined the family timber company. He served for a short time as Hon Treasurer of OCGS, and in 1978 was elected Hon Secretary in succession to Peter Wreford-Brown. John threw himself into the affairs of OCGS with unique enthusiasm, energy and generosity. A *bon viveur* and wine buff (he was for 30 years the Hon Director of the Guild of 19 Lubricators, a dining club raising money for charity), he liked to share his enjoyment with Old Carthusian golfers. On arrival at an OC golf event, they would frequently find, supplied by John, an early morning glass of champagne to get the day off to a good start. And when OCGS met with success, he liked to celebrate by organising and hosting a dinner or lunch.

On one occasion in the 1980s, John organised transport for the Halford Hewitt team and supporters from Sandwich to a restaurant some distance away. The transport turned out to be a coach equipped with both a bar and a barmaid. Henry Longhurst, one of the passengers, sipping vodka at the back, remarked that it was the most vulgar thing he had ever known, but added that he was enjoying it hugely.

John was married to Linda, Curtis Cup golfer in 1988 and an international player and England Captain. Their house Middle Cottage, immediately behind the 4th green at Royal St George's, Sandwich, has become a base for the Charterhouse Halford Hewitt team and their supporters. Following the destruction by fire of the hotel in Deal where the team previously stayed (acidly described by Peter Ryde, the OC Golf Correspondent of *The Times*, as 'one of the six worst hotels I have stayed in during 30 years of travel'), the Baymans have provided or arranged nearby accommodation, and supplied unique hospitality. As Ryde wrote in *The Carthusian*, 'at Middle Cottage the Carthusian spirit is warmly and carefully fostered; differences are laughed away, individual quirks are tolerated, even encouraged; bruised egos are massaged, swollen ones deflated. Hangovers, if there are any, are of the highest class. Everyone remotely connected with the Carthusians is greatly in debt to John and Linda Bayman'. Since John's death in 2005 following a series of health problems, Linda and their family have continued to this day to make their unrivalled contribution to OCGS.

John served as the non-playing Halford Hewitt Captain for three years from 1986, and was Captain of OCGS from 1996–2001.

…and as *bon viveur*. At Hoylake GC for the 1992 Curtis Cup, having travelled up after watching the Derby at Epsom.

The Bayman Jug, presented in memory of John Bayman as the trophy competed for in an annual match between Royal St George's GC, Sandwich, and OCGS.

John Bayman as golfer…

M J Christmas b. 1939

In 1960, Martin Christmas established himself at the age of 20 as one of the country's leading amateur golfers. A former Boys and Youths International, in that year he reached the 36-hole final of the English Amateur Championship at Hunstanton, losing only at the 41st hole after the longest final in the history of the Championship. He also tied for the English Open Amateur Stroke-Play Championship (the Brabazon Trophy) at Ganton. Later in the same year, he was selected to play for England in the Home Internationals, and he continued to play in these every year until 1964.

In 1961, Christmas reached the semi-final of the British Amateur Championship at Ganton. He also reached the semi-final in 1964 and 1965, as well as the quarter-final in 1963. In 1961, he was a member of the ill-fated GB & I team at Seattle in the last Walker Cup to be played by 36-hole matches of foursomes and singles. The team suffered a crushing 14–1 defeat, but Christmas had the distinction of being the only GB & I winner, his victory in the singles saving the GB & I team's score from being a complete daisy-chain. He was also a member of the 1963 team at Turnberry. In his only match in the event, he lost in the first round of singles matches to the mercurial but highly-talented Bill Joe Patton, destined the following year to finish only one stroke behind Ben Hogan and Sam Snead (who tied) in the US Masters after finding a ditch and taking 6 at the 71st hole. Christmas was also a member of the GB & I team in the Eisenhower Trophy (the World Cup) in Japan in 1962, and in the bi-annual European Championships in 1960, 1962 and 1964. He retired from serious competitive golf in 1965, after qualifying as a Chartered Surveyor, but nevertheless won the Belgian Amateur Championship in 1974 (being surprised to find the name of Jeremy Sutherland Pilch already on the trophy).

For OCGS, Christmas has been an ever-present and inspirational figure, as well as a leading player in Charterhouse teams. He is

Martin Christmas playing in the Worplesdon Mixed Foursomes in 1961.

50 years later, Christmas watches the Halford Hewitt at Deal in the company of *left* team member Simon Stilwell.

a Halford Hewitt 'centenarian', having played in 121 matches for Charterhouse between 1959 and 2000, and been a member of six winning teams; and he has subsequently been the non-playing Halford Hewitt Captain from 2001 to 2003. He has also been a member of winning teams in the Grafton Morrish, the Queen Elizabeth, the Bernard Darwin and the Senior Bernard Darwin tournaments, and was the President of OCGS from 2004 to 2009. A former captain of Royal Mid-Surrey GC and President of the Surrey County Golf Union, he is currently the Vice-President of the Public Schools' Golfing Society (responsible for organising the Halford Hewitt), and is due to take over as President in the near future.

P J W Benka 1946–2007

As a young man Peter Benka was an outstanding amateur golfer. Although previously a Boy and Youth International and a Surrey county player, he first came into national prominence in 1967 when, still aged only 20, he was the leading amateur in the Open Championship at Hoylake. In the same year he also won the 72-hole British Youths Amateur Championship, leaving several notable players in his wake, and repeated that success the following year. In the same two years he also won the Surrey Amateur Championship, and in 1967 won the County Champions' Championship. He was selected to play for England in the Home Internationals in 1967-68-69-70. He also played for GB & I in the 1969 Walker Cup match in Milwaukie, winning two and halving one of his four matches. Peter also won several other international honours and prestigious amateur events, including the Dutch Amateur Championship in 1972.

Peter Benka made his first appearance for Charterhouse in the Halford Hewitt in 1965, when still aged only 18, and played regularly for 36 years in 107 matches. He was a member

The swing of Peter Benka. For the full finish see p.62.

of the Cup-winning side in seven years, including the three years 1982–83–84, when he was the successful Charterhouse Halford Hewitt captain.

As well as being a stylish and skilled golfer, Peter was genial and modest man, and a popular and highly regarded personality. He had a distinguished career as a stockbroker. A loyal Carthusian, he served on the Governing Body of Charterhouse, and was much involved in the creation of the Halford Hewitt golf course at the School.

It was typical of Peter Benka that he gave much back to golf, as a senior figure and administrator. He served on the Surrey Committee for over 25 years. From 1981 onwards he also served on various Committees of the English Golf Union. He was an England Selector for several years, being the Chairman of Selectors from 1994 to 1998. At the date of his untimely death from cancer, he was the President-elect of the English Golf Union, and only weeks away from taking office.

In 1971, Peter married Pam Tredinnick, a Curtis Cup player in 1966 and 1968, and the GB & I Curtis Cup captain in 2002. Their son Mark was the Oxford golf captain and since 1993 has been a prominent member of the Charterhouse Halford Hewitt side. He has already played over 60 matches, and bids fair to surpass his father's number.

Secretaries and Treasurers

The responsibilities and duties of the Honorary Secretary of OCGS, as of any other Golfing Society, are onerous and time-consuming. The Rules of OCGS provide for the Hon Secretary to be elected annually. The Rules also require the election annually of an Hon Treasurer but, as is commonly provided in the rules of similar societies, the same person can fill both roles. This obviously requires that person to shoulder a good deal of additional work and responsibility. But the responsibilities of the two offices often overlap, and there must necessarily be a good deal of communication and consultation between the two. This is saved if one person holds both offices, and some Hon Secretaries have preferred to serve as the Hon Treasurer also.

OCGS has been exceptionally fortunate with its Hon Secretaries. There have been only 12 in the whole 100 years of its existence. The writer is able to testify that the last seven have, without exception, all fulfilled their obligations (of course undertaken voluntarily) with manifest enthusiasm, efficiency and good humour. From all accounts, the same seems to have been also true of each of their five predecessors.

J L F Vogel 1872–1943

The first Hon Secretary was Julius Vogel. The son of a former Prime Minister of New Zealand, he was a founder of OCGS, and was given the initial responsibility of circularising all members of 'the Old Carthusian Football and Cricket Club' (later renamed the Old Carthusian Club) and inviting them join the new Society. Later, after he had ceased to hold office, Vogel presented the Society

Julius Vogel, as a member of the Charterhouse Shooting VIII at Bisley, 1891.

with a 'Burmese Bowl' which is the Vogel Seniors Challenge Bowl, now competed for at the Spring Meeting by players aged 55 and over. Vogel was assisted by the first Hon Treasurer, Edwin Cawston, referred to earlier (see pp.10–11).

A N Howard 1891–1959

The surviving records of the Society are unfortunately silent as to the years of the First World War and the years immediately following, and it is uncertain when Vogel and Cawston gave up their offices. But by 1923, A N (Alexander) Howard had become Hon Secretary and Treasurer, and as mentioned earlier (see pp.24–26) was the person responsible for the running of the first Halford Hewitt Tournament in 1924. Shortly after that Tournament had been completed, however, Howard went abroad on business and felt compelled to resign. T C Bower undertook the arrangements for the 1924 Autumn Meeting. Howard presented the Cup which bears his name, competed for at the Spring Meeting by players with handicaps of 12 and above.

Bernard Drew 1892–1971

Howard was succeeded as Hon Secretary and Treasurer in 1925 by Bernard Drew, who held the office until 1927 and again for a short time in 1947. Drew was a well-known and successful amateur golfer in the 1920s, reaching the final of the French Amateur Championship in 1922. He played in the first Halford Hewitt match in 1924 (held at Stoke Poges GC, where he was then Captain) and then regularly up to 1929. After a gap of six years, he also played in the 1935 final against Shrewsbury, stepping in for Victor Longstaffe and partnering Gerry Weare. They won their match, helping Charterhouse to a 4–1 victory.

In 1930, Bernard Drew was appointed the Secretary of Royal Cinque Ports GC, Deal, (at an initial salary of £350 per annum). Apart from some of the War years, he remained in that office

Bernard Drew, when Secretary of Royal Cinque Ports GC, Deal in the 1930s.

until 1950. During that time he was responsible for the many arrangements required for the Halford Hewitt and other events. He also saw the Club through the difficulties which faced the Club after the War, as well as the restoration of the golf course following the two severe floods which took place in 1938 and 1949. He was a popular and much respected figure. After leaving Deal, he served as the Secretary of Sunningdale GC from 1950 to 1960. During that period, he was the Captain of OCGS from 1954 to 1959, and also the Halford Hewitt Captain from 1955 to 1957.

C F Woodbridge 1891–1955

Cyril Woodbridge became Hon Secretary and Treasurer in 1929 and continued in those offices until 1947. He also was a fine golfer, and played regularly in the Halford Hewitt between 1925 and 1936, being a member of five winning teams. He also played occasionally thereafter, including once as a substitute in an early round in 1949. He was Captain of OCGS from 1949 to 1954. He was also the playing Captain of the winning Halford Hewitt team in 1935, but (as mentioned previously) dropped himself from the later rounds because he considered that he had lost his form.

Cyril Woodbridge, when Captain of Royal Mid-Surrey GC in 1932. See also the Mel cartoon on p.16.

A P Bristowe 1902–78

Alan Bristowe succeeded Bernard Drew as Hon Secretary and Treasurer in 1927 and served for two years. He was elected just after he had played in the Halford Hewitt earlier in the year. He won all three of his matches, but did not play again, although he was nominated as a reserve in several years. He resigned in 1929, say the Minutes, 'because he was getting married'. Whether that is a good and sufficient reason for resigning may be a matter of debate. But at least the marriage produced his younger son Gerald, who became a leading player and figure in OCGS and was then Secretary of the Public Schools' Golfing Society from 1959 to 1966.

Alan Bristowe *Hon Sec OCGS 1927–1929* and Gerald Bristowe (aged 14) on their way to winning the Fathers and Sons Tournament at West Hill GC in 1949. They were chaperoned by the tweed-suited Mrs Babs Bristowe, wife and mother, complete with handbag held Margaret Thatcher-style, ready to deal firmly with any opposition to her menfolk. Gerald Bristowe has the unique record of having played in the Tournament with five different partners, having also competed with each of his four Carthusian sons.

Carthusians Richard and son Simon Barrow later also won the Fathers and Sons Tournament (see p.121). Another Carthusian pair, Julian Hill and son Archie, reached the final in 2010. David Comer with his father also won the Tournament in 1958 whist still at Charterhouse, and had to miss playing in the Gerald Micklem because of a clash of dates. Michael Bryant won the Tournament with his father in 1965, but unlike the other Carthusian winners had left Charterhouse several years previously.

O E Evans 1907–81

Owen Evans took over as both Hon Secretary and Hon Treasurer in 1947, and remained in that office until 1959. A stockbroker, he was an enthusiastic and cheerful figure who managed the affairs of OCGS with great efficiency and an easy charm. Those who were young at the time remember him with much affection. After retiring as Hon Secretary, Evans remained an active figure in OCGS, and became Captain in 1962 to 1964 and subsequently President from 1969 to 1972.

Owen Evans

P G Wreford-Brown 1910–91

Peter Wreford-Brown was a member of the extensive Carthusian family mentioned previously (see pp.12–13). At Charterhouse, he was a contemporary in the same House as Henry Longhurst and Eric Prain, both future Cambridge golf captains and Halford Hewitt players. He did not have their golfing skills, but shared their enthusiasm for the game. After a career as an Army officer, he was appointed Secretary at Worplesdon GC in 1958 and subsequently held other similar posts.

Peter Wreford-Brown became Hon Secretary of OCGS in 1959, combining that office with Hon Treasurer. He served for 16 continuous years, missing only a part of one year when he enjoyed a sabbatical and John Shipton took over. He then became President of OCGS from 1975 until 1979.

Peter Wreford-Brown

J E Bayman 1932–2005

John Bayman has been featured at pp.108–9.

N A C Moore b. 1949

In late 1982 John Bayman, then both Hon Secretary and Hon Treasurer, decided that he would like a separate Hon Treasurer to collect the subscriptions and manage the financial affairs of OCGS. He also determined that Nick Moore, a Chartered Accountant who was a Halford Hewitt player and a prominent member of OCGS, would fit the role admirably. Moore had been a member of the Committee for some years, but in January 1983 made the mistake of being late for a Committee Meeting. A short time after arriving, he was informed that he had already been unanimously selected for appointment as Hon Treasurer. As the Minutes put it, 'N Moore reluctantly agreed the appointment'. So began a long treasurership, with different Hon Secretaries (including himself), which ended only when Moore was elected Captain of OCGS in 2002. The Minutes record that Moore's appointment had resulted in the correct subscriptions having been collected for the first time for many years, with a consequent increase in the Society's funds. So Bayman's judgment was amply justified.

As Hon Treasurer, Moore was much involved in the financing of the construction of the Halford Hewitt golf course at the School. Then, when Bayman retired as Hon Secretary in 1986, Moore took over that office also, continuing as Hon Treasurer. He was the Hon Secretary at the date of the opening of the Halford Hewitt golf course at Charterhouse, and was much involved in organising and managing the celebrations and events of the day.

Nick Moore, then Hon Secretary OCGS, finds that he does not have enough hands when organising the golf which followed the opening of the Halford Hewitt course in 1988.

Peter Goodliffe

P G Goodliffe b. 1958

Peter Goodliffe, a member of a strong Carthusian family, was a Halford Hewitt player during the 1980s. He took over from Nick Moore as Hon Secretary of OCGS in 1989, continuing until 1995. He has also served as the Halford Hewitt Captain since 2010. Goodliffe has also been the Captain of OCGS since 2011, and during his period of office he will undertake the busy and responsible duties of captaincy in the OCGS Centenary year 2012.

S R Barrow b. 1936

Simon Barrow's father, Brigadier Richard Barrow, a Carthusian who was the Secretary of Royal St George's GC, Sandwich, had played once in the Halford Hewitt in 1951, winning his match although Charterhouse lost in the first round. Simon played in the Halford Hewitt in 11 years between 1959 and 1976. In all those years, the distinction between Simon and his father has escaped the compliers of the official Halford Hewitt records, and he has there been accorded the same military rank and appears continuously as 'Brig S R Barrow'.

Simon Barrow in his Halford Hewitt years.

After 1960, Simon Barrow spent some years in Australia. When he returned in 1966, Peter Ryde, the Carthusian golf correspondent of *The Times*, in his preview of the Charterhouse prospects in the Halford Hewitt wrote that they were 'playing with renewed confidence' [partly] 'thanks to the return from a spell in Australia of Barrow, a strong hitter who has settled well into a partnership with Christmas', and added that 'Christmas's game is at present in the weekend category but on that level he is a strong support'. This extract, with its suggestion that Martin Christmas would be a mere support player for him, has been treasured by Barrow and has kept him warm during the cold winters. However,

Brig Richard Barrow and son Simon at the Fathers and Sons Tournament at West Hill GC in 1952, which they won.

Ryde's comments were (in a sense) proved correct, for Barrow and Christmas won all six of their matches together in that year, contributing greatly to Charterhouse winning the Tournament, and altogether won 12 of their 15 matches as partners.

Barrow became Hon Secretary of OCGS in 1995, only giving up in 2005 on being appointed Hon Treasurer of the Old Carthusian Club.

J A S Gill b. 1944

After holding the position of Hon Treasurer of OCGS for three years, John Gill took over from Simon Barrow as Hon Secretary, as well as continuing as Hon Treasurer. One would have thought that these were sufficient responsibilities for any one man, but remarkably Gill for seven years acted also as the Hon Secretary and Hon Treasurer of his profession's golfing society, the Chartered Accountants GS. He will be the Hon Secretary and Hon Treasurer of OCGS during the Centenary year, with the heavy responsibility of introducing financial realism into some of the more extravagant ideas for suitable celebrations.

John Gill

Membership, Meetings and Matches

OCGS Membership

Naturally enough, membership of OCGS is in general confined to Old Carthusians. But from the earliest days, the Rules have allowed for the election of Honorary Members who are not Old Carthusians. Several members of Brooke Hall and others with strong connections to the School or OCGS have been elected in this category.

The number of members of OCGS has fluctuated over the years. The initial invitation in 1912 to Old Carthusians to join the newly-formed OCGS produced 143 members, but by 1926 (partly as a result of a post-War drive to recruit new members), this number had risen to 328. There was a further increase to over 400 by the early 1930s, perhaps as a result of the publicity given to the Charterhouse wins in the Halford Hewitt in that period. A drive to recruit more members in 1933 was reported to have attracted 121 new members, including the Chief Justice of Grenada, HH the Maharaja of Indore and a schoolmaster in Buenos Aires who sent a Promissory Note for £1 in respect of his subscription 'pending the alteration of the rate of exchange'. By 1938, the number of members had risen to a record 776.

The numbers naturally declined during the 1939–45 War. However a circular letter sent to Old Carthusians in 1947 resulted in over 90 new members, and by 1948 the numbers had risen back up to 728.

Since these heady days, the number of members has declined for several reasons, (including perhaps the inevitable increase in the rate of subscription, for many years only £1 per annum.) The latest membership list includes the names of 362 members.

The Ladies

The introduction of girls as pupils at Charterhouse in the early 1970s was certain, sooner or later, to lead to applications by ladies to join OCGS. This prospect was viewed with apprehension by some. At the time, similar questions were arising in many other old school and professional golfing societies. Some were fully opposed to lady members, and suggested that eligible ladies should be invited to form their own society. Some were grudgingly inclined to accept lady members, but voiced concerns about which tees they should play off at meetings, their handicaps, and so on, and wished to impose conditions. Some considered that lady members should be fully accepted without conditions. After a good deal of prevarication, virtually all societies in the end fully accepted lady members – and have lived happily ever afterwards. OCGS was to be no exception.

The matter was first discussed by the Committee in 1979, and the Minutes record: 'The possibility of eligible Lady Old Carthusians applying for membership was discussed. It was decided after lengthy discussion to await such an application'. At the AGM later in the year, 'the possible election of eligible Lady Members was raised and whilst opposing views were expressed the President [Jock Moss] asked for time to review the Society's Rules'. Shortly afterwards, a respected senior member made an application for his daughter to join. It might have been thought that this would result in an early decision, but that did not happen, and there was further prevarication. At the 1980 AGM there was a 'lively discussion' and the Committee was asked to 'investigate further and make recommendations' to be considered at the next AGM. The Minutes record a 'short sharp discussion' at the 1981 AGM, when it was agreed that 'any female Old Carthusians were quite in order to create an OC Ladies Golfing Society which may or may not meet concurrently with the gentlemen as circumstances dictated'. This unedifying stance was maintained for several more years, and, although it was conceded that ladies could join OCGS, they were not encouraged to attend meetings.

The matter finally came to a head in late 1994, when (say the Minutes) the question of lady members was 'once again' raised in Committee and there was 'much debate'. However, a respected senior member, Patrick Shovelton, stated that 'having discussed the matter at every Committee meeting for the last three years, [he] was getting fed up with going round in circles. Carthusians were Carthusians whether they were male or female and he could not understand what all the fuss was about'. This argument won the day. A proposal that ladies should be allowed to play in all competitions was put to the vote and carried with one dissentient. Since then, ladies have been welcomed as members and at Meetings, but sadly their numbers have so far been low.

Linda Bayman, Honorary Member of OCGS.

One advantage of allowing lady members is that it is possible to elect a lady as an Honorary Member. Linda Bayman has for many years welcomed Old Carthusian teams to her home and acted as a most generous dinner hostess and OCGS supporter. She has been duly elected as the first lady Honorary Member.

OCGS Meetings

Apart from the War years and immediately afterwards, Spring and Autumn Meetings have been held every year. There are the usual scratch and handicap singles events, and also foursomes events. All were for many years decided by medal scores or in 'bogey' competitions, but are now played under the more popular and satisfactory Stableford scoring system.

The Spring Meeting takes place over two days. It was formerly played over both days of a weekend, but now is played as one singles round on a Friday afternoon and two foursomes rounds the following day. A black tie dinner is held on the Friday evening, at which a draw is made for partners for the following morning's foursomes, usually with a form of selling sweep on the result. The competitions are played for several trophies presented by former OCGS members mentioned earlier in this book. The Friday singles competition is played for the Halford Hewitt Scratch Challenge Cup, the Cawston Challenge Cup as the handicap trophy, the Alexander Howard Challenge Cup (handicaps over 12), and the Vogel Seniors Challenge Bowl (players aged 55 and over). So golfers of all abilities and ages are catered for. The Saturday foursomes are played for the Ben Travers and Victor Longstaffe Cups.

The Autumn Meeting is played on one day with a singles round in the morning and a foursomes round in the afternoon, for similar trophies, and there is also a Ladies' Shield. In addition, the Owen Evans Gold Medal is presented for the best aggregate scores in the two Meetings.

The Spring Meeting was in the past held at several different golf courses both in the London area and more distant. In 1927 it was held abroad, at Le Touquet. The green fee for the whole weekend was 15/-, and the *en pension* cost of The Golf Hotel, Le Touquet (where the 1927 AGM was held) was £1 per day. More recently,

An unusual view of the driveway and entrance to the Clubhouse of Royal St George's, Sandwich, a frequent venue for the OCGS Spring Meeting.

the Meeting has usually been held outside the London area, frequently at Royal St George's, Sandwich, but also at Aldeburgh, Deal, Littlestone, Woodhall Spa, and other venues. In 1949, the Meeting was held at Formby, with the intention of attracting more competitors with homes in the North. But this venture was unsuccessful, because there was only a small entry and most players came from the South anyway.

The Autumn Meeting has in the past also been held at a variety of courses, but in recent years has been held at The Berkshire. It is a popular and usually well-attended event.

Matches

One of the stated purposes of the foundation of OCGS was to play matches against other golfing societies and clubs. This purpose has been amply fulfilled. 2011 was a typical year in this respect, and the Fixture List for that year shows that 16 matches were played. These were of two kinds. First, there were matches played off scratch, which are treated as trials for the Halford Hewitt. These were against Littlestone GC, Old Rugbeian GS, Woking GC, Old Etonian GS, Royal St George's GC and Royal Cinque Ports GC, all played in the early part of the year, and against Rye GC played in October. The Rye fixture, which is of long-standing, is played by keenly contested foursomes over two days and is an eagerly awaited and enjoyable occasion.

The second kind of matches are played on handicap, and so available to be enjoyed by golfers of varying skills. There were seven matches against old school societies, and matches against Littlestone GC and the School.

The Fixture List also mentions the Alba Trophy at Woking, the Hector Padgham Trophy at Royal Ashdown Forest and the Royal Wimbledon Putting Competiton. The Alba Trophy is a strongly contested team competition, and was won in 1975 by Iain Quick, Peter Benka and Michael Hughesdon representing OCGS.

Golf at Charterhouse and the Halford Hewitt golf course

It might reasonably have been thought that the success of Charterhouse in the Halford Hewitt in the 1930s was attributable to the opportunities and facilities for playing golf at the School. But this was emphatically not the case. The *Who's Who* entry for the late Sir Osbert Sitwell included: '*Educ:* during the holidays from Eton'. Older generations of Carthusians, if asked when they learned to play golf, might well have replied similarly 'during the holidays from Charterhouse'. For until the 1950s, there were no facilities at all at the School for playing, coaching or practising golf. Any boy keen enough had to bicycle, with his bag of clubs slung over his back, to one of the nearest golf courses at Puttenham, Enton Green (Royal West Surrey GC) or Bramley, all some miles away. Even if he was able to hang on to the tail of lorry for part of the journey, in the manner described by Henry Longhurst in his *My Life and Soft Times*, this was a tiring and hazardous enterprise, undertaken by only a handful of boys.

Moreover, some of the authorities at the School did not approve of golf, considering that a boy's time was better spent playing some team sport. In substance, they agreed with an Old Carthusian clergyman who in 1908 wrote in a letter to *The Observer*: 'It does not give me any pleasure to read that an Old Carthusian has distinguished himself at golf or billiards'. Even if he did not consider those two games as inventions of the Devil, he plainly regarded proficiency at either as the proverbial sign of a mis-spent youth. Even as late as 1946, the School's 'Games Committee', comprising the Headmaster and a few masters and senior boys, opined that 'golf was not a suitable game for a school society'. As the Old Carthusians had won the Halford Hewitt seven times in the 1930s, including the last Tournament before the outbreak of the 1939–45 War and so were the current holders of the Cup, this seems a surprising viewpoint.

However, it should not be thought that all in authority at Charterhouse were negative about golf. A 1908 issue of *The Carthusian* contained not only a spirited reply to the reverend gentleman's letter to *The Observer*, but also the results of an 8-aside golf match played at Puttenham that year between Brooke Hall (the Charterhouse masters) and the School. Among those playing for the School were Alexander Howard, later Hon Secretary of OCGS and in that capacity responsible for the organisation of the first Halford Hewitt Tournament in 1924, and F E Pegler, who played in that Tournament. Later records are sparse, but a report in *The Carthusian* of a similar match (the first after the 1939–45 War) played at New Zealand GC on the first day of the Easter holidays in 1949 suggests that other similar matches had been played in the 1920s and 1930s. Later several similar matches were played at different courses, as well as foursomes matches between OCGS and pairs of masters and boys.

The Gerald Micklem Trophy

In 1953, Gerald Micklem, a Walker Cup player and future captain, wrote a letter to Graham Pratt, who had recently been a semi-finalist in the Boys' Championship (and was then Captain of the Football XI), inviting Charterhouse to compete in a tournament he was inaugurating. This was to be a knock-out tournament between teams of five players from each school, to be played at Woking GC in the following Easter holidays. The first Gerald Micklem tournament was held in April 1954. After defeating Bradfield in the first round Charterhouse were defeated by Rugby, although Pratt himself duly won his match with some excellent figures. This contest saw early appearances of two young boys destined to become Walker Cup golfers, Martin Christmas (then aged 14) for Charterhouse and Michael Attenborough for Rugby. They played

The Charterhouse team at the first Gerald Micklem tournament 1954.
Seated IJR Aitchison   HC Cairns   GE Pratt *Captain*   NSP Rowe   MJ Christmas
Standing OE Evans *Hon Sec OCGS*

against each other, but their match was left unfinished, Rugby having secured the necessary three points for a win.

Charterhouse have competed in every subsequent Gerald Micklem, and won it on seven occasions. The first two wins were in 1963 and 1964, when Peter Benka was a team member. These were followed by wins in 1983, 1987, 1989, 1992 and 1994, when other future Halford Hewitt players competed.

The Start of Coaching and Matches

In the 1950s, some golf coaching started to become available, with a professional, who was partly funded by the School and partly by the Golf Foundation (created to encourage schoolboys to learn golf), attending once a week to give lessons. After a while, these were held on the playing field known as Broom and Lees or in a net inside the pavilion of the cricket ground Maniacs. After matches against other schools had been commenced in 1968, one hour of each session was reserved for team members, while another hour was available to others, of any standard. In addition, some boys managed to play some golf at Hankley Common GC at a cost of two shillings (10p) a round, getting transport to that club with a cadet corps truck taking other boys sailing at Frensham.

The first match played against another school, apart from the Gerald Micklem Trophy, did not take place until 1967. It was an unofficial match against Eton at Hankley Common, kept secret from the School authorities, and was won 5–0 by Charterhouse. However, the Headmaster, Oliver Van Oss (a keen golfer who had played in the matches against OCGS), happened to learn about the match from an Eton master at a social occasion. Nick Moore, who had organised the match, was summoned by Van Oss who formally warned him not to do it again, but expressed total delight with the result.

This unofficial match seems to have prompted a change in the attitude to matches against other schools, because in 1968 matches were played against Eton, Wellington and Bradfield. From then on fixtures were arranged against several other schools. Anthony Rowan-Robinson, a housemaster and himself a good golfer, became the first 'Master in charge of golf'. He has been succeeded by, in turn, Tony Wreford-Brown, Andrew Wilson, Stephen Shuttleworth, Richard Lloyd and Catherine Robinson. All of them have contributed greatly to the development and enjoyment of golf at the School.

Andrew Wilson

Stephen Shuttleworth

Rev Richard Lloyd

A Century of Charterhouse Golf

School golf team 1987.

Standing JD Taylor
TPC Bonner   AR Wilson
Master SJG Wilkinson
CAM Ayres

Seated/kneeling
TA Bristowe   C Peters
TDL Orgill   RV Mumford
AR Powell   MSP Benka

School golf team 1991.

Standing SJ Shuttleworth
Master RG Lloyd
OAC Wright   NJ Martin
AR Wilson *Master*

Seated JB Tanter
CAM Ayres   MSP Benka
BP Mote

The Halford Hewitt golf course

The main fillip to golf at Charterhouse has been the construction and establishment of the 9-hole golf course at the School. For this credit must go to OCGS and those who contributed to the cost, and in particular and principally to Nicholas Royds.

Royds had played in the Halford Hewitt, the Grafton Morrish and the Queen Elizabeth Tournaments. He had also been a considerable and generous benefactor to OCGS, making himself responsible for some of the costs involved in sending teams up to Edinburgh for the Queen Elizabeth, for the preparation and dispatch of circulars to OCGS members, and for other expenses. In 1979, he began his five-year captaincy of OCGS. During that period, he initiated proposals for the construction of a golf course at Charterhouse. Stowe had long had a 9-hole course, Harrow had recently constructed one, and it was known that other schools were either constructing or proposing to construct similar courses. Royds considered that Charterhouse, with its strong golfing tradition, should have a similar course and that OCGS should take the leading role in such a project. He was keenly supported by the President of OCGS, Jock Moss. Moss was then a Governor of the School, and so formed a valuable link between OCGS and the School's Governing Body.

With the approval of the OCGS Committee, Royds therefore obtained in 1982 the advice of Donald Steel, a leading golf course architect and former Halford Hewitt opponent, as to the feasibility of creating a 9-hole golf course on a part of the School's land, farmed during the War and known as 'Farm', which was then unused. Steel considered that proposed area would be eminently suitable. It was in a beautiful position, formed an attractive and convenient compact area, and had several established trees and other useful natural features. Relatively little earth-moving would be needed, nearly all confined to the construction of greens, tees and bunkers. Steel proposed that the course should be suitable for all grades of golfer, without big carries, but at the same time be

Golf architect Donald Steel beside one of his greens under construction.

demanding and interesting enough for the better players. He also produced some preliminary estimated costings.

These proposals for a golf course were well received by the School and the Governing Body. But at the time there was an ongoing intention that, if planning permission could be obtained, the playing field area Broom and Lees might be sold for housing development, which would mean that the playing fields there would have to be relocated to the area of the proposed golf course. There was also an impending change of Headmaster. These factors led to the golf course proposal being shelved for over two years. However in November 1984, the Committee was informed that Broom and Lees had been designated as Green Belt land, so that the golf course area would no longer be required for playing fields and the project could proceed.

Royds thereupon indicated his willingness to continue with the project and to start raising funds. The Committee agreed with his initial suggestion that the construction costs should be shared equally by the School and OCGS. But this suggestion proved unacceptable to the Governing Body, because the School had other funding priorities. It became clear that the whole construction cost, plus the costs of a watering system for the tees and greens, of greenkeeping machinery and other items, would have to be borne by OCGS. Royds set about raising funds to meet that cost. This was to be done through the Carthusian Trust, a charitable organisation, mainly by use of four-year covenants which were then necessary for gifts to be tax-efficient. After lunches hosted by Royds with some key potential donors, about half of the required amount was covenanted.

Nicholas Royds, Captain OCGS 1979–1984, poses on a newly constructed green at the opening of the Halford Hewitt course 1988.

Aerial view of the Halford Hewitt golf course at Charterhouse, taken shortly after the course was opened in 1988. Note the school buildings, including the modern Houses in the background.

Douglas Miller, Captain OCGS 1984–1988 at the opening of the Halford Hewitt course 1988.

Royds was greatly assisted in these matters by Douglas Miller, who had succeeded him as Captain of OCGS in 1984 and by Nick Moore, newly elected as Hon Treasurer. They undertook most of the administrative work involved, and were also both involved in the negotiations with the School.

A meeting was held in May 1986 with the Chairman (Richard Thornton) and other representatives of the Governing Body. The Headmaster Peter Attenborough, who was very supportive of the project, was also present. Royds expressed confidence that OCGS would be able to raise sufficient money over a four-year period and would offer to donate the whole of the construction and other costs. He also offered to the Governing Body his personal guarantee to back the OCGS offer. Richard Thornton said that he thought that these were remarkable and generous offers, which indeed they were. On this footing, it was agreed that it would be recommended to the full Governing Body that the project should go ahead and that the future maintenance of the course should be the permanent responsibility of the School, and this was subsequently confirmed by the Governing Body.

So in 1986, the construction of the golf course, to Donald Steel's design, was commenced. At the same time, Royds held further lunches for potential donors. Later, over 300 circular letters were sent by Nick Moore to all OCGS members. The final amount raised by these means was £163,240, from 97 contributors.

The golf course was completed in 1988. The course is named the Halford Hewitt course in memory of OCGS's most famous name, and the individual holes are also named in accordance with suggestions by some of the contributors. The 1st is called Oakroyd, a tribute to Nick Royds. The 2nd is named after John Sunley, whose Trust was a substantial contributor. 'Jock Moss', 'Beck', 'Longhurst' and 'Morrison' are named after distinguished OCGS members, and 'Rookery Nook' is one of Ben Travers' best known plays.

Old Carthusian Golfing Society 1912–2012

OFFICIAL OPENING
of the
HALFORD HEWITT GOLF COURSE
by
Mr. Denis Thatcher, MBE, TD.

CHARTERHOUSE　　Saturday July 2nd, 1988

Top Denis Thatcher cuts the tape to open the Halford Hewitt golf course, aided by OCGS Captain Gerald Bristowe. The luncheon marquee is in the background.

Above Denis Thatcher hits the first tee-shot at the opening of the Halford Hewitt course, and Gerald Bristowe and most of the gallery anxiously watch the flight of a high slice. Remarkably, the ball finished inside the luncheon marquee.

Peter Alliss also tees off at the opening of the Halford Hewitt course. Note the persimmon-headed wooden driver.

The Halford Hewitt golf course was officially opened on Saturday 2nd July 1988 by Denis Thatcher, husband of Margaret Thatcher (then Prime Minister). A Champagne Reception was followed by luncheon in a large marquee erected next to the first hole of the course. Speeches were made by Gerald Bristowe, the new Captain of OCGS, Richard Thornton, Denis Thatcher and Peter Alliss, then Captain of the Professional Golfers Association and the father of a Carthusian. Denis Thatcher hit the opening drive off the first tee, as a prelude to a competition, involving nine groups of three players making a 'shotgun start' off the other tees.

There have been two alterations to the Halford Hewitt course since its construction and official opening. The first alteration was made to allow for the building of part of a new sports hall, and involved the relocation of first tee and a re-alignment of the first hole. The second alteration has taken place in

Mark Benka aged 15 on the Halford Hewitt golf course soon after its opening in 1988.

2011, and was made necessary in order to provide space for part of a new artificial hockey pitch. One hole has been replaced by a new hole constructed, again to Donald Steel's design, on other land provided by the School. The overall result is considered to be an improvement to the course.

Present day School golf

Coaching sessions continue to be held once a week, still on Broom and Lees, and the Halford Hewitt course is used for a number of competitions involving players of all ages and standards. In addition, like any other golf course, the Halford Hewit course is played on for ordinary games and practice during most of the year, although play is severely restricted by the lack of daylight in the two winter Quarters after British Summer Time has ended. Over 20 matches are played against other schools during the year, at Senior, Under 16 and Yearling levels. While the home Yearling matches usually take place on the Halford Hewitt course, matches at the more senior levels are played over an 18-hole course, now usually at Worplesdon GC. Members of the more senior teams are able to join a Junior Membership scheme at that Club.

Catherine Robinson who since the beginning of 2011 has been the 'Master in charge of golf' at Charterhouse. Catherine holds the distinction of being the first lady to play in the Halford Hewitt, having been a member of the Westminster side from 2001 to 2006.

Dinners and social events

When an occasion has occurred which justifies a celebration of some kind, such as an anniversary or success on the golf course, the almost invariable practice of OCGS is to hold a dinner. As mentioned elsewhere, a black tie dinner has been held annually on the evening of the first day of the Spring Meeting, but some of the special celebration dinners should be mentioned.

21st and 25th Anniversary Dinners 1933 and 1937

These were the first Anniversary Dinners to be held by OCGS. Both took place at the Savoy Hotel (a favourite venue for OCGS dinners). There are few records of either Dinner, and it is not known who were the speakers. There were no pre-War Halford Hewitt celebration dinners, probably because the lengthy lunch after the final, which was then played on the Monday morning and was attended by the players and supporters of both teams, was considered sufficient.

50th Anniversary Dinner 1962

OCGS celebrated its 50th anniversary in 1962, and it was clear that this should be celebrated in the usual way by a dinner in London. At the Annual General Meeting held at in 1960, the Captain, Owen Evans, put forward alternative suggestions as to the kind of dinner which should be held. One suggestion was that the dinner should be a grand social occasion, with several official guests as well as private guests of members. This suggestion was preferred, by a vote taken at the Meeting, to a more limited occasion with only members and a few official guests. The Hon Secretary, Peter Wreford-Brown, was asked to investigate suitable venues and obtain prices.

Wreford-Brown reported the result of his investigations to the Committee. He gave his opinion that the most suitable venue would again be the Savoy Hotel, where there could be a reception, with drinks and canapés in the Abraham Lincoln Room, and the dinner in the Manhattan Room. The Savoy had quoted the most expensive price of all the possible venues, but nevertheless the Committee decided to hold the dinner there. The modern reader will rub his or her eyes in disbelief and wonder if this sentence contains a misprint, but the price of the Savoy dinner, inclusive of all the reception drinks and the wines on the table, was £3/15/- per head.

So the dinner was duly held at the Savoy, on Friday 2nd November 1962. The President, Gerry Weare, presided at the Dinner and proposed the Loyal Toast. The first speaker, who proposed the health of OCGS, was Raymond Oppenheimer, a former Walker Cup Captain and a prominent golf administrator. The inimitable Ben Travers (featured at pp.96–98) replied on behalf of the members. He was followed by Sir Anthony Hawke, the Common Sergeant (the senior Judge at the Old Bailey) and a member of the Society, who proposed the health of the guests. The Headmaster of Charterhouse, Brian Young, replied on behalf of the guests. There were 12 official Society guests, and 32 other private guests also who attended.

By all accounts, and judging by some of the letters of thanks received, the dinner was an enjoyable success. It was also a financial success. The Hon Secretary, Peter Wreford-Brown reported to the next Committee meeting that there was a shortfall of only £7/14/8d, and there was one account outstanding. He considered that OCGS could easily bear this loss.

Peter Wreford-Brown stayed overnight at the Savoy. Again this is hard to believe, but his total bill amounted to £11/5/10d. This did not include the cost of his dinner, but it did include 'Tea, Coffee, Sandwiches, Fruit etc' (5/6d), 'Garage, Petrol etc' (£1/3/6d), 'Breakfast' (16/6d) and some drinks (£1/10/-), as well as the cost of the room (£6/10/-).

Halford Hewitt Celebration Dinner 1974

The winning of the Halford Hewitt in 1974 merited a Celebration Dinner, again at the Savoy, later in that year, presided over by the President, Derek Drayson. Ben Travers again made a characteristically amusing first speech. He was followed by Henry Longhurst, who simply said he could not possibly match that and immediately sat down. He was however prevailed upon by the diners to continue, so with a show of reluctance he rose to his feet again and delivered an excellent speech, full of his usual dry humour.

Ben Travers toasts the health of the Society at a celebratory dinner at the Savoy Hotel in 1974. Seated on his left are Derek Drayson, *President OCGS* (reaching for his glass) and Sir Anthony Hawke. In the foreground stands the Halford Hewitt Cup.

Grafton Morrish Celebration Luncheon 1976

To celebrate the winning of the Grafton Morrish, a Luncheon was held, once more at the Savoy Hotel, on Friday 26th November 1976, with the members of the successful team and a number of invited guests present. It is not recorded whether anyone present did any work in the afternoon, but after champagne, two fine wines and port to accompany a mouth-watering menu, it seems unlikely.

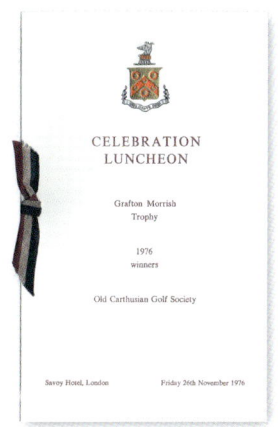

The winning 1976 Grafton Morrish team in celebratory mood even before the Luncheon had begun.

Standing: PJW Benka   IA Quick   MH Bradley   MJ Christmas   ANC Royds
Seated: MC Bryant   RS Gilbert Scott *GM Captain*   RV Braddon

Triple Celebration Dinner 1982

During 1982, Old Carthusian cricket, football and golf teams were all successful so Charterhouse became the holders of *The Cricketer* Cup, the Arthur Dunn Cup and the Halford Hewitt Challenge Cup at the same time. This achievement was celebrated by a dinner held in November, on this occasion at Old Charterhouse.

Just under 100 were present, the majority being members of OCGS. The President of OCGS Jock Moss presided, and the Captain Nick Royds proposed the health of the guests. The other speakers were Gerald Micklem, Donald Steel and the cricket writer E W Swanton.

75th Anniversary Dinner 1987

This was held at a different venue, the dignified Old Hall of Lincoln's Inn.

Halford Hewitt & Bernard Darwin Celebration Dinner 1999

The winning in 1998 of both the Halford Hewitt, in an emotional final, and the Bernard Darwin gave ample justification for that year's Captain John Bayman to engage once more in his favourite activity of organising an OCGS celebration dinner. This was held on the 13th January 1999, and originally intended to be at Boodle's. However, the room at that Club was found to be insufficient to accommodate the numbers wishing to attend, and the venue was switched to the Old Hall of Lincoln's Inn. Bayman himself was one of the speakers and delivered his usual entertaining and amusing speech.

100th Anniversary Dinner

This is planned to take place in June 2012 (after the publication of this book), again in the Old Hall of Lincoln's Inn.

Other events

Apart from these and other formal functions, OCGS members have been the recipients of considerable private hospitality from a number of members. At the risk of offending (and with apologies to) other generous hosts, mention should be made of Halford Hewitt who entertained Carthusian teams, in particular at his home near Bury St Edmunds when they played matches at Royal Worlington; of John and Linda Bayman, previously mentioned; and of Jock Moss, who hosted several dinner parties and other functions for OCGS teams.

Party hosts Jock and Oz Moss entertain at their party for some OC golfers. Pam Benka is in the background.

Guests Gerald Bristowe, Graham Pratt and Ian Woolley.

Appendix 1
individual Halford Hewitt results

(1) Figures in brackets denotes matches won or lost at the 19th or a later hole.
(2) 'Halved' denotes agreed halves when the overall outcome of the match had been determined, and a more accurate expression might be 'unfinished'.
(3) 'NRR' denotes no recorded result in the archives.

SURNAME	INITIALS & NAME	YEARS PLAYED	FIRST YEAR	LAST YEAR	MATCHES PLAYED	WON	LOST	HALVED	NRR
ADAMS	G M (George)	3	1933	1938	11	9	2	–	
AGATE	G J (Jeffrey)	7	1953	1964	20	8	9(1)	3	
ASPREY	G H E (George)	1	2006	2006	3	2	1	–	
AYRES	C A M (Christian)	13	1993	2011	43	26(1)	7	10	
BAILHACHE	W J (William)	1	1974	1974	2	2	–	–	
BARNETT	J R (John)	3	1970	1972	10	9	1	–	
BARROW	Brig R (Richard)	1	1951	1951	1	1	–	–	
BARROW	S R (Simon)	11	1959	1976	39	26	11(1)	1	1
BATHURST	A W (Andrew)	6	1986	1992	14	5	5(1)	4	
BECK	J B (John)	27	1925	1959	92	53(5)	31(1)	1	7
BENKA	M S P (Mark)	19	1993	2011	64	44(2)	15(2)	5	
BENKA	P J W (Peter)	36	1965	2001	107	69(4)	28(6)	10	
BIDWELL	R W (Richard)	8	1980	1989	27	17(1)	8	2	
BOOTH	E T C (Edward)	1	1925	1925	2	2	–	–	
BOURN	T A (Dale)	16	1924	1939	62	40(1)	18(2)	4	
BOWER	A G (Alfie/Baishe)	1	1924	1924	1	–	1	–	

SURNAME	INITIALS & NAME	YEARS PLAYED	FIRST YEAR	LAST YEAR	MATCHES PLAYED	WON	LOST	HALVED	NRR
BOWER	T C (Theodore)	3	1927	1929	11	6(1)	5(1)	–	
BRADDON	K V (Ken)	6	1938	1951	20	14	3	2	1
BRADDON	R V (Richard)	21	1960	1983	71	49(1)	15(1)	7	
BRADLEY	M H (Malcom)	4	1975	1978	6	3	3	–	
BRIGGS	J R (James)	2	1952	1955	3	–	1	–	2
BRISTOWE	A P (Alan)	1	1927	1927	3	3	–	–	
BRISTOWE	G R (Gerald)	17	1952	1973	48	27(1)	16(2)	1	4
BRUCE	W W (William)	3	1925	1929	8	7	–	1	
BRYANT	M C (Michael)	24	1954	1979	78	51	19(1)	5	3
BULL	C F (Cecil)	1	1925	1925	2	1	1	–	
BURDON-SANDERSON	R L (Lionel)	5	1930	1936	24	19(2)	5	–	
CALDWELL	R I C (Richard)	10	1998	2010	36	23	10	3	
CHRISTMAS	M J (Martin)	40	1959	2000	121	81(1)	32(1)	7	1
COMER	D D S (David)	7	1961	1975	28	17	8	3	
COX	A J (Alan)	14	1953	1974	43	27	9	5	2
DRAYSON	D A (Derek)	13	1948	1973	47	28(1)	13(1)	3	3
DREW	B (Bernard)	7	1924	1935	15	9(1)	6(1)	–	
EVANS	O E (Owen)	1	1949	1949	1	1	–	–	
FLOOD	H (Harry)	2	2006	2008	4	1	3(1)	–	
FOLEY-BRICKLEY	P J (Patric)	19	1980	2007	59	34(2)	18(1)	7	
FORBES-WATSON	R D (Dick)	6	1949	1954	16	7	4	2	3
FREARSON	K (Karl)	3	1985	1994	6	2	4	–	
GAMBLE	R M (Roddy)	2	1983	1984	12	6	3	3	
GIRDLESTONE	G R (Gathorne)	2	1926	1927	5	3	2(1)	–	
GOODLIFFE	P G (Peter)	6	1980	1990	11	5(1)	3	3	
GREENLY	J O H (John)	4	1955	1958	13	6	6	–	1
HILL	R J (Julian)	23	1957	2011	76	44	27(2)	5	

SURNAME	INITIALS & NAME	YEARS PLAYED	FIRST YEAR	LAST YEAR	MATCHES PLAYED	WON	LOST	HALVED	NRR
HOLLINGSWORTH	A P (Andrew)	4	2008	2011	15	7	5	3	
HOLLINS	A H (Allatt)	1	1929	1929	4	2	1	1	
HOOMAN	C V L (Charles/Chubby)	6	1926	1938	20	13	7(1)	–	
HUGHESDON	M C (Michael)	24	1969	1999	76	54(5)	19(3)	3	
HUMPHRIES	G N P (Gerald)	4	1924	1931	9	4	5		
HUMPHRIES	R P (Percy)	2	1924	1926	3	1	2(1)	–	
JACKSON	G P (Pat)	2	1931	1932	6	5	1	–	
LADENBURG	A L (Arthur)	1	1925	1925	2	1	1		
LANGFORD	G M (Michael)	18	1962	1980	49	34(1)	14	1	
LE BAS	H E (Ernest)	4	1924	1928	10	5	5(1)	–	
LLOYD	A S (Angus)	5	1977	1983	16	7	5	4	
LONGHURST	H C (Henry)	14	1934	1956	56	39	8	6	3
LONGSTAFFE	V C H (Victor)	10	1924	1934	24	18	6(1)	–	
MANNING	R F (Robert)	10	1996	2010	33	19(1)	9(2)	5	
MARSTON	J P (John)	2	1930	1931	6	5	1	–	
McKINNIA	R G M (Ryan)	1	2009	2011	14	10	4(1)		
MIDDLETON	C V (Cecil)	11	1933	1951	52	36(1)	12	3	1
MILLER	D B (Douglas)	3	1954	1973	8	3	3	–	2
MOORE	N A C (Nick)	6	1979	1985	27	15	8	4	
MORRISON	J S F (John)	17	1924	1948	66	49	12(1)	4	1
MORRISON	R G (Roggie)	2	1930	1932	6	4	2	–	
MOTE	B P (Barnaby)	17	1995	2011	61	35	20(1)	6	
MURDOCH	T R (Tim)	5	1968	1973	11	6	4	1	
MUTCH	W G (Warren)	4	2006	2011	11	5(1)	4(1)	2	
NEEDHAM	P W G (Peter)	14	1948	1964	44	23	14	3	4
NESBITT	M W (Michael)	2	1955	1956	4	1	2	1	
O'BRIEN	I M (Michael)	1	1979	1979	1	–	1	–	
ORGILL	T D L (Tim)	16	1991	2011	55	39(2)	14(1)	2	

SURNAME	INITIALS & NAME	YEARS PLAYED	FIRST YEAR	LAST YEAR	MATCHES PLAYED	WON	LOST	HALVED	NRR
PEGLER	F E (Francis)	1	1924	1924	1	–	1	–	
PHILLIPS	R C (Robin)	3	1989	1992	5	1	3	1	
POWELL	A R (Andrew)	1	1990	1990	3	1	2	–	
PRAIN	E M (Eric)	13	1928	1951	50	32(1)	15(2)	2	1
PRATT	G E (Graham)	1	1968	1968	2	1	1	–	
QUICK	I A (Iain)	23	1972	1996	69	36	25(2)	8	
ROBINSON	M J C (Michael)	1	1990	1990	2	–	2	–	
ROYDS	A N G (Anthony)	5	1976	1982	19	12(3)	6(3)	1	
ROYDS	D J G (David/Jumbo)	13	1983	1996	39	21	17(1)	1	
ROYDS	N C (Nicholas)	11	1957	1970	33	18(1)	13	1	1
SCOTT	R S Gilbert (Dickie)	40	1953	1992	128	81(6)	33(2)	11	3
SMITH	A (Anthony)	1	2003	2003	2	1	–	1	
SMYTHE	P C (Patrick)	1	1932	1932	1	1	–	–	
SNELLING	A G (Alan)	4	1929	1948	20	14	5	–	1
STANLEY	A T H (Alex)	4	2008	2011	8	3	4	1	
STILWELL	S J (Simon)	15	1996	2011	57	34(1)	15(1)	8	
SUTHERLAND PILCH	J G (Jeremy)	11	1967	1991	38	26	11(1)	1	
TATE	R D (Rupert)	4	2002	2005	21	10(1)	4	7	
THOMPSON	J H (Jack)	19	1930	1963	74	48(2)	18	4	4
WAGSTAFF	E A (Ewan)	2	1950	1952	3	–	1	–	2
WEARE	A G (Ted)	4	1954	1969	12	5	5	–	2
WEARE	F G C (Gerry)	15	1932	1961	62	44	12(1)	4	2
WHITE	C G (Christopher)	3	1986	1994	5	1	3(1)	1	
WHITE	P H F (Pat)	17	1933	1956	58	38	12(1)	5	3
WILLIAMS	Col A E (Alfred)	1	1924	1924	1	–	1	–	
WOODBRIDGE	C F (Cyril)	13	1925	1938	39	27	10(1)	2	
WYBAR	M J P (Michael)	1	1972	1972	1	1	–	–	

Appendix 2
Halford Hewitt gold medals

OCGS members who have won two or more gold Halford Hewitt medals awarded to members of the winning team.

No. of medals	Name
8	JB Beck JSF Morrison JH Thompson
7	PJW Benka TA Bourn
6	MJ Christmas HC Longhurst EM Prain RS Gilbert Scott FGC Weare CF Woodbridge
5	RV Braddon RL Burden-Sanderson MC Hughesdon CV Middleton PHF White
4	IA Quick
3	SR Barrow MC Bryant VCH Longstaffe NAC Moore
2	MSP Benka RW Bidwell AJ Cox MC Croft RIC Caldwell DA Drayson RJ Hill CVL Hooman RM Gamble GM Langford AS Lloyd BP Mote DJG Royds SJ Stilwell J Sutherland Pilch

Appendix 3
winners of scratch cups

SPRING MEETING
From 1914 Halford Hewitt Challenge Cup

1912   WW Bruce
1913   CF Woodbridge
1914   Capt J Harvey
1915–1919   *Not played*
1920   B Drew
1921   CVL Hooman
1922   CVL Hooman
1923   AN Howard
1924   B Drew
1925   B Drew
1926   CF Woodbridge
1927   TA Bourn
1928   GM Adams
1929   RB Beare
1930   FGC Weare
1931   CF Woodbridge
1932   JSF Morrison
1933   JB Beck
1934   CF Woodbridge
1935   JHA Clarke
1936   CF Woodbridge
1937   JSF Morrison
1938   JSF Morrison
1939   EH Chambers
1940–46   *Not played*
1947   JB Beck
1948   JD Forbes-Watson
1949   CF Woodbridge

AUTUMN MEETING
From 1959 Bristowe Cup

For many years there was no scratch event at the Autumn Meeting. After the morning 'bogey' competition had been replaced by a Stableford competition, a scratch event was introduced in 1959. Gerald Bristowe presented a Cup which he had inherited as the trophy, and was himself the first winner.

SPRING MEETING		AUTUMN MEETING	SPRING MEETING		AUTUMN MEETING
1950	JH Thompson		1984	PJW Benka	MC Hughesdon
1951	PWG Needham		1985	IA Quick	MJC Robinson
1952	GR Bristowe		1986	RS Gilbert Scott	K Frearson
1953	DB Miller		1987	RS Gilbert Scott	PJ Foley-Brickley
1954	FGC Weare		1988	RS Gilbert Scott	RS Gilbert Scott
1955	JB Beck		1989	PJ Foley-Brickley	IA Quick
1956	JB Beck		1990	RS Gilbert Scott	JG Lennox
1957	DA Drayson		1991	PJW Benka	JJ Pearmund
1958	AG Weare		1992	JK Divett	RFC Ladenburg
1959	GR Bristowe	GR Bristowe	1993	RS Gilbert Scott	IR Woolley
1960	JB Beck	MJ Christmas	1994	RM Gamble	RJ Hill
1961	RV Braddon	RS Gilbert Scott	1995	RS Gilbert Scott	NAC Moore
1962	JB Beck	DA Drayson	1996	IA Quick	MJ Christmas
1963	JB Beck	TR Murdoch	1997	GM Langford	MSP Benka
1964	AS Lloyd	JC Moss	1998	RF Manning	IA Quick
1965	PF Braithwaite	NC Royds	1999	MJ Christmas	NAC Moore
1966	GM Langford	RS Gilbert Scott	2000	DM Innes	NAC Moore
1967	GM Langford	DHG Goodliffe	2001	DM Innes	JJ Pearmund
1968	J Sutherland Pilch	RS Gilbert Scott	2002	MJ Christmas	NAC Moore
1969	MC Hughesdon	MJ Branfoot	2003	C Spencer-Phillips	RJ Hill
1970	PJdeQ Adams	RS Gilbert Scott	2004	MJ Christmas	SJ Stilwell
1971	IA Quick	JC Moss	2005	RJ Hill	MJ Christmas
1972	RS Gilbert Scott	RS Gilbert Scott	2006	PJW Benka	AS Lloyd
1973	DA Drayson	RS Gilbert Scott	2007	DM Innes	DM Innes
1974	RS Gilbert Scott	IA Quick	2008	MSP Benka	DDS Comer
1975	RS Gilbert Scott	RS Gilbert Scott	2009	RJ Hill	TJ Drayson
1976	*No record*	GM Langford	2010	RCD Lawson	WG Mutch
1977	*No record*	IA Quick	2011	NAC Moore	WG Mutch
1978	*No record*	MC Hughesdon			
1979	RS Gilbert Scott	MC Hughesdon			
1980	RS Gilbert Scott	RS Gilbert Scott			
1981	RS Gilbert Scott	RM Illingworth			
1982	RS Gilbert Scott	NF Gay			
1983	RS Gilbert Scott	RJ Walker			

Appendix 4
OCGS Officers

Presidents

1912–13	Lord Alverstone
1913–27	Rev GS Davies
1930–47	Maj-Gen Sir HC Lowther
1947–49	Halford W Hewitt
1949–54	VCH Longstaffe
1954–60	Ben Travers
1960–63	FGC Weare
1963–66	JB Beck
1966–69	HCD Whinney
1969–72	OE Evans
1972–75	DA Drayson
1975–79	Brig PG Wreford-Brown
1979–86	JC Moss
1986–98	RS Gilbert Scott
1998–2004	GE Pratt
2004–09	MJ Christmas
2009–	RM Gamble

Graham Pratt, OCGS Captain 1992–95 and President 1998–2004.

Roddy Gamble, Captain OCGS 1995–98 and President 2009–.

Secretaries

1912–14	JLF Vogel
1914–1923	*No record*
1923–25	AN Howard
1925–27	B Drew
1927–29	AP Bristowe
1929–47	CF Woodbridge
1947–48	B Drew/OE Evans
1948–59	OE Evans
1959–75	PG Wreford-Brown (1963–64 with JK Shipton)
1971–75	PG Wreford-Brown
1975–86	JE Bayman
1983–83	JE Bayman
1986–89	NAC Moore
1989–90	NAC Moore/PG Goodliffe
1990–95	PG Goodliffe
1995–2003	SR Barrow
2003–06	SR Barrow
2006–	JAS Gill

Treasurers

	E Cawston
	No record
	AN Howard
	B Drew
	AP Bristowe
	CF Woodbridge
	B Drew/OE Evans
	OE Evans
	PG Wreford-Brown
	JE Bayman
	JE Bayman
	NAC Moore
	NAC Moore
	NAC Moore
	NAC Moore
	SR Barrow
	JAS Gill
	JAS Gill

Captains

1912–14	Prince Albert of Schleswig-Holstein	1970–72	GM Adams
1914–1923	*No record*	1972–74	HMO Knox
1923–25	C Wreford-Brown	1974–76	FL Perkins
1925–27	Sir Hugh Bray	1976–79	RS Gilbert Scott
1927–47	Halford W Hewitt	1979–84	NC Royds
1947–49	VCH Longstaffe	1984–88	DB Miller
1949–54	CF Woodbridge	1988–91	GR Bristowe
1954–59	Bernard Drew	1992–95	GE Pratt
1959–62	HCD Whinney	1995–98	RM Gamble
1962–64	OE Evans	1998–2001	JE Bayman
1964–66	DA Drayson	2001–04	NAC Moore
1966–69	JC Moss	2004–07	PJW Benka
1969–70	BR Bearman	2007–10	MHG Boswell
		2010–	PG Goodliffe

Michael Boswell, OCGS Captain 2007–10.

Halford Hewitt Captains

1925–27	CVL Hooman	1979	GR Bristowe	1996–2000	RM Gamble (n/p)
1928–31	VCH Longstaffe	1980–85	PJ W Benka	2001–03	MJ Christmas (n/p)
1932–33	JSF Morrison	1986–88	JE Bayman (n/p)	2004–05	RJ Hill
1934–35	CF Woodbridge	1989–90	MC Hughesdon	2006–07	NAC Moore (n/p)
1936–37	JB Beck	1991–94	DJG Royds	2008–09	RJ Hill
1938–39	TA Bourn	1995	J Sutherland Pilch (n/p)	2010–	PG Goodliffe (n/p)
1947	FGC Weare				
1948–49	JH Thompson				
1950	EM Prain				
1951	HC Longhurst				
1952–3	JB Beck				
1954	PHF White				
1955–57	B Drew (n/p)				
1958–60	RS Gilbert Scott				
1961–62	GR Bristowe				
1963	DA Drayson				
1964	MC Bryant				
1965–70	RS Gilbert Scott				
1971–72	MC Bryant				
1973–74	JC Moss (n/p)				
1975	MC Hughesdon				
1976–78	GE Pratt (n/p)				

Julian Hill, Halford Hewitt Captain 2004–05 and 2008–09.

Author's notes

As I have mentioned in the Preface on p.6, both Bernard Darwin and Henry Longhurst sometimes appear to have relied entirely on their memories and not to have consulted either their contemporaneous reports or the record books when they came later to write reminiscences.

Thus, in an amusing passage in his *Golf Between Two Wars* about Chubby Hooman's singles victory in the first Walker Cup match (which I have quoted verbatim), Darwin states that Hooman won at the 37th hole with 'a sparkling three'. But in *The Times*, he had reported merely that Hooman's opponent Jesse Sweetser was 'heavily bunkered'; and Sweetser later stated that in trying to drive the green, he had hit his ball into a car-park. A four from Hooman was good enough, and neither mentions him getting a three, sparkling or otherwise. In addition, Darwin describes an epic encounter in the Halford Hewitt between Charterhouse and Winchester (again, I have quoted the passage verbatim), but he dates it in the last year before the War, when it was manifestly in 1937.

In the chapter headed 'Some Modest Success' in his *My Life and Soft Times*, Henry Longhurst wrote that that in the last six years before the 1939–45 War, Charterhouse won the Halford Hewitt five times and in the other year were in the semi-final; but in fact Charterhouse did not even reach the quarter-final in 1938. He also stated that, playing in the bottom Charterhouse pair with the redoubtable John Morrison, they lost only one match, and that was when the result had already been decided; but the Hewitt records show that, although they enjoyed great success, they in fact lost on three occasions in that period. There are other errors, including the mis-naming in a photograph caption of Cyril Woodbridge, who had been the Hon Secretary of OCGS and a fellow Halford Hewitt team member for many years. One commentator has averred that 'Longhurst seldom got things wrong'; but that is not so.

The same chapter contains Longhurst's account of how Halford Hewitt came to present his Cup. However, Longhurst was still a schoolboy at the time, so (as he himself makes clear) his account could only reflect what he had been told several years later. Puzzlingly, he does not mention 'Susie' Mellin at all, but says that the other person concerned with John Beck was the distinguished surgeon Harold Gillies. Among the likely sources of Longhurst's information would almost certainly have been John Morrison and probably also Bernard Drew. In 1939, Morrison edited a collection of articles on golf in a book *Around Golf*. One of the articles concerned the Halford Hewitt and was co-written by Bernard Drew. This mentions Mellin, but lends no support to Longhurst's account. If that account has any substance, it is surprising that there is no hint of it in *Around Golf*. In his book on the Halford Hewitt *A Festival of Foursomes*, Peter Ryde expressed his doubts about Longhurst's account. Those doubts were amply justified.

about the author

Nigel Hague arrived at Charterhouse during Hitler's War. Already a keen golfer, he found that there was virtually no golf played at the School, notwithstanding the pre-War success of Charterhouse in the Halford Hewitt. He can remember playing only one round, when one of the chaplains, Rev John Rutherford, kindly sacrificed part of his meagre petrol ration to take a small party of boys to Bramley GC.

After National Service, he went up to Pembroke College, Cambridge where, after an initial dalliance with Mathematics, he read Law. Among other activities, he also sometimes played golf in the lower order of the Stymies, the University second team. He was called to the Bar in 1956 and appointed Queen's Counsel in 1981. From 1987 until his retirement in 2000, he was a Circuit Judge.

In 1968 he made his first venture into authorship when he wrote a legal text-book *Hague on Leasehold Enfranchisement*, which has become the leading text-book on an obscure but occasionally important topic. This is now in its fifth edition. He was solely responsible for an expanded second edition, but the later editions have been entirely the work of others. He is uncertain whether being edited in one's lifetime is a mark of honour or shame.

Nigel has been Captain of Denham Golf Club, of which he has been a member since boyhood, and of the Bar Golfing Society. For the latter he wrote a centenary history *Wigs on the Links* in 2003, and for Denham wrote *A Centenary Portrait* in 2009.

His enthusiasm for golf has not been matched by his skill, but he is one of several Carthusians who never played in the Halford Hewitt but have represented the School in the Bernard Darwin and the Senior Darwin Tournaments. He currently manages the Charterhouse side in the Very Senior Darwin and occasionally plays as an emergency reserve.

Index

Figures in italics indicate a photograph or other image. Figures in bold type indicate a featured section. This index covers only pages 8–147 (and not the Foreword, Preface, Appendices *et seq*).

Adams, GL   36, *39*, *53*, 56, *58*
Addington (The) GC   25, 39
Agate, GJ   49–50, 56–7
Aitchison, IJR   130
Alba Trophy (Woking GC)   127
Albert of S-Holstein, Prince   11, 16, **18–19**
Aldeburgh GC   27, 37, 126[7]
Aldwych Theatre, London   96
Alliss, P (Peter)   140
Alverstone, Lord (Sir R Webster)   11
Ampleforth College   52
Anderson Scales   77
Armstrong, Wally (US golfer)   35
Arthur Dunn Cup (Football)   17, 23–4, 28, 146
Attenborough, M J   129
Attenborough, P (Headmaster)   138
Ayres, CAM   71–2, 75, 80, 82, *132*
Bar Golf Tournament   94
Barnato, Woolf (racing driver)   104
Barnett, JR   58–9
Barnton see Royal Burgess GS
Barrow, Brig R (Richard)   117, 120, *121*
Barrow, SR (Simon)   54–5, 57–8, 59, 69, 71, *117*, 120–1, *122*
Bathurst, AW (Andrew)   65, 66
Bathurst, PJ (Peter)   66
Bayman, JE   65, 68, 81, **108–9**, 119, 146–7
Bayman, Mrs Linda   *7*, 68, *109*, *125*, *147*
Beck, JB   25, 27, 33, 37–9, 42–4, 46–7, 50, 52–4, 58, 94, 99, **102–3**, 138
Benka, MSP (Mark)   52, 67, 68, 69, 70, 71, 72, 73, 75, 77, 81, 82 ,*113*, *132*, 140
Benka, Mrs Pam   *113*, *147*
Benka, PJW (Peter)   52, 55, 57–8, 59, 60, 61, 62, 64, 65, 66–8, 69, 71, 79, 81–2, 87, 91, **112–3**, 127, 130, 145
Berkshire (The) GC   127
Bernard Darwin Tournament   **88–91**, 146
Bidwell, RW   62, 65, *81*

Bonner, TPC   *132*
Boswell, MHG   75, *155*
Bolton School   81
Bourn, TA (Dale)   *5*, 27–8, 37, 42–3, *44*, 45–6, **104–5**
Bower, AG   27, **29**, 100
Bower, TC   29, *115*
Braddon, KV (Ken)   36, 46, 47–8, 49, 57, *89*,
Braddon, RV (Richard)   56–8, 59, 61, 62, 79, *85*, *145*
Bradfield College   64, 70, 129, 131
Bradley, MH   *145*
Braid, James (pro golfer)   39
Bramley GC   128
Bristowe, AP (Alan)   **116–7**
Bristowe, Mrs Babs   *117*
Bristowe, GR (Gerald)   49–50, *51*, *53*, 54, 56–7, *85*, 116, *117*, *139*, 140, *147*
Bristowe, TA   *132*
Brookmans Park GC   96
Bruce, WW   *9* 10
Bryant, MC   49–50, 52, *53*, 54, 56–8, 65, 79, *85*, 117, *145*
Buchan, Charlie (footballer)   101
Bull, CF   33
Burden-Sanderson, RL   36–7, 39, 42, 44
Cairns, HC   130
Caldwell, RIC   68, 69, 71, 72–3, 75
Canford School   8
Carr, JB (Joe)   66
Cawston, E   *9*, *10*, 11, *15*, *115*
Chapman, APF (cricketer)   97
Cheltenham College   8, 34
Chigwell School   8
Christian of S-Holstein, Prince   **18–9**
Christmas, MJ   52, 54, 55, 56–8, 59, 60, 61–2, 65–6, 68, 69, 71, *85*, 90–1, **110–1**, 120, *129*, *130*, 145
City of London School   8
Clare College, Cambridge   35, 94, 105
Clifton College   8, 73–4, 76

Colt & Alison (golf architects)   101
Comer, DDS   56, *117*
Corinthians FC   29, 100
Cox, AJ   49, 50, 52–4, *57*, 59, 90, 91–2
Cranleigh School   8
Crieff High School   87
Croft, MC (Michael)   68, 69, 71, 86, 87
Cumberland Lodge, Windsor   18
Darwin, Bernard (golf writer)   *6*, 27, 33, 35, 38, 41, 44, 46, 48, 99
Davies, Rev GS   11
Davis, JPL   92
Deal see Royal Cinque Ports GC
Drayson, DA   36, 47–8, *53*, 54, 56–8, 81, 89–90, 91, *144*
Drew, B (Bernard)   23, 25, 28, *34*, 36, 42, 50, *53*, 93, *115*
Dulwich College   62, 70
Dunn, Arthur (footballer)   17
Edinburgh Academy   50, 71
Epsom College   72
Eton College   24, 27, 33, 38, 42, 50, 56, 131
Evans, OE (Owen)   16, 47–8, 50, *53*, 56–7, *58*, *89*, *107*, 118, *130*, 142
Faldo, MH   75
Fathers and Sons Tournament   117, 121
Fergusson, S Mure   *20*, 21
Fettes College   55, 56
Foggo, Mrs Carol (Royal Burgess GS)   86
Foley-Brickley, PJ   66, 68, 69, 71, 72, 82, *86*, 87
Forbes-Watson, RD   48
Forgan, AD   84
Formby GC   127
Fownes, Bill (US golfer)   99
Gamble, RM   63, 64, 69, 71, 90, 91, 92, *154*
Garnett, E   10–11
Garnett, RM   98
George Heriot's School   82

158

Gilbert Scott *see* Scott
Gill JAS 7, *75*, 122
Glasgow Academy 87
Glasgow High School 87
Goodliffe, DHG (Derek) 66
Goodliffe, PG (Peter) 62, 74, *75*, 77, 120
Grace, Dr WG (cricketer) 17, 18, 97
Grafton Morrish Tournament 8, 23, 56, 69, 78–83, 84, 145
Grafton, Peter 78, *83*
Greenly, JOH *50*, 53
Griffiths of Govilon, Lord H 88
Guilford Hotel, Sandwich Bay 37
Gupta, A 90
Haberdashers' Aske's Boys' School 79
Haileybury School 55, 81
Halford Hewitt (the man) *see* Hewitt
Halford Hewitt Captains 31–2
Halford Hewitt Golf Course 108, 119, **133–141**
Halford Hewitt Tournament 8, **22–77**, 78–9, 84–5, 88, 102, 128–9, 144, 146
Hankley Common GC 131
Hardwick Hall, Bury St Edmonds 93
Harrow School 34, 39, 41, 43, 45, 46, 49, 52, 53, 59, 66, 77, 81, 90, 91, 106, 133
Harvey, Capt J 10
Hawke, Sir A 143, *144*
Herd, Alex/Sandy (pro golfer) 39
Hewitt, CdeL 93
Hewitt, Halford W 11, *14*, 15, 21, 24–6, 28, 34, 39, *41*, 44, 45, **93–6**, 147
Hewitt, Halford W (senior) 93
Hewitt, Sir Thomas KC 93
Highgate School 8
Hill, AJB 75, 117
Hill, RJ (Julian) 7, 65, 66, 68, 69, 71, 74–5, *82*, 86, 87, 117, *155*
Hinman, JC 90
Hollingsworth, AP 74, 75
Hooman, CVL 27, 33, 39, **98–99**
Howard, AN 23–6, **115**, 129
Hughesdon, MC 61–2, 64, 65, 66, 69, 90, 127
Humphries GNP (Gerald) 27
Humphries RP (Percy) 27
Hunstanton GC 37, 78, 82
Hutchinson, HG (Horace) **20–21**
Hymers College 80
Jolly, WH (pro golfer) 39
Kent County Cricket Club 99
Lacey, AJ (pro golfer) 39

Ladenburg, A 33
Langford, G M 7, *55, 56, 58, 79–80, 90–1*
Le Bas, H E 28
Le Touquet GC (France) 126
Lehman, Tom (US golfer) 35
Lincoln's Inn, London 146
Littlestone GC 127
Lloyd, AS (Angus) 59, 61
Lloyd, Rev R (Richard) *131–2*
Longhurst, HC 26, 35–6, 41, 43–4 47–8, 49, 52, 93, 97, 101, **105–6**, 108 118, 128, 138, 144
Longstaffe, VCH *27*, 28, 36, *37*, 38, 41–42, *47–8*, 93, 101, 115
Loretto School 50, 61
Ludgrove School 17
Malvern School 24, 33, 57, 64, 72,
Manning, RF 71, *72–3, 74–75*, 75, 76, 86, 87
Marlborough College 58, 59, 72
Martin, NJ *132*
McKinnia, RG 73, 74, 75–6
Mellin, GL ('Susie') 23, 25, 28
Merchant Taylors' School 72, 82
Merchiston Castle School 71
Micklem, GH 129, 146
Middle Temple, London 94
Middleton, CV 36, 40–2, *43–4*, 45, *47–8*, 49
Miller, DB *56, 58, 85, 90, 91, 138*
Moles GS 28
Moore, NAC 7, *58*, 61, *63*, 64, 71, 81, 91–2, 119, 120, 131, 138
Morrish, Peter 78
Morrison, JSF (John) 18, 27–9, 38–40, 44, 45–6, *47–8*, 52, 53, 66, **100–2**, 104, 106, 138
Morrison, RG (Roggie) 18, 38, 102, 104
Moss, J C *32*, 53, *56–8, 65, 81*, 93, 133, 138, 146, *147*
Moss, Mrs Oz *147*
Mote, B P 68, 69, *71–2, 132*
Mumford, RV *132*
Murdoch, TR 80
National Links, Long Island, USA 99
Needham, PWG *47–8*, 49, 56–7
Nesbitt, MW 50
Newbolt, Sir H (poet) 76
New Zealand GC 21, 129
Nicholson, BTG 56
Noble, RA (Master) 21
Oppenheimer, RH 143
Orgill, TDL 70–1, *72–3, 75*, 77, 86, 87, *132*

Owen, N (Hon Sec PSGS) 73, 76
Oxford and Cambridge GS 8
Oxhey GC 16
Padgham, AH (pro golfer) 39
Patton, WJ (US golfer) 110
Pearmund, JJ *92*
Pegler, FJ 27–8, 129
Perry, Alf (pro golfer) 39
Peters, C *132*
Plowright, Joan (actress) 96
Powell, AR *132*
Prain, EM 34–5, 38, 42, 44, 45, *47–8*, 49, 118
Pratt, GE 69, *75, 82, 83,* 129, *130, 147*
Princes' GC, Sandwich 37, 43
Public Schools' GS 16, 25, 78, 96, 116
Public Schools Old Boys GA 78, 79, 83, 111
Puttenham GC 128–9
Queen Elizabeth etc Tournament **84–87**
Quick, IA 7, 59, 61–2, 65, 66, 69, 71, 80, *81–3*, 127, 145
Radley College 64
Repton School 61
Robinson, Catherine 131, *141*
Robinson, MJC *92*
Robson, Fred (pro golfer) 39
Rossall School 49, 53, 72
Round FH (Master) 11
Rowan-Robinson, GA (Master) 131
Rowe, NSP *130*
Royal & Ancient GC 21, 88, 102–3
Royal Ashdown Forest GC 127
Royal Burgess GS, Barnton 84, 86
Royal Cinque Ports GC, Deal 22, 26, 28, *30*, 96, 102, 115, 127
Royal High School, Edinburgh 85
Royal Mid-Surrey GC 16, 111, 116
Royal North Devon GC 20
Royal St George's GC, Sandwich 21, 30, 102, 109, *126*
Royal West Norfolk GC, Brancaster 78, 80
Royal West Surrey GC 128
Royal Worlington GC 93
Royds, ANG (Anthony) 59, 61, *145*
Royds, DJG (David/Jumbo) 64–5
Royds, NC (Nicholas) 53, 55, *56–7, 79–80, 85*, 133, *135*, 138, 146
Rugby School 38, 42–3, 48, 127, 129
Russell, Rev J (Headmaster) 20
Rydal School 80
Ryde, Peter (OC golf writer) 120
Rye GC 37, 127

Saunders RM (Royal Burgess GS) 32
Savoy Hotel, London 56, 97, 142–5
Scott, Sir Giles Gilbert 108
Scott, RS Gilbert (Dickie) 5, 7, 49, 50, 53–8, 59, 61–2, 65, 69, 79–82, 85, 90, 91–2, 96–7, **106–8**, 145
Senior Bernard Darwin Tournament 91–2
Sherborne School 80
Shipton, JK (John) 56, 118
Shipton WK (Bill) 68, 69
Shovelton WP 125
Shrewsbury School 42, 62, 64–5, 67–8, 80, 115
Shuttleworth, SJ (Master) 131–2
Skegness GC 15
Skene, Col PGM (R&A) 103
Smith, GO 10, **17**
Snelling, AG 36, 46, 47
Spenser-Phillips, C 91–92
Stanley, ATH 75
Steel, DMA 37, 55, 59, 133, *134*, 138, 141, 146
St Peter's School, York 80
Stilwell, SJ 68, 69, 71, 72, 73, 75, 85, 111
Stockport School 82
Stoke Poges (Stoke Park) GC 15, 27, 115
Stowe School 55, 133
Sunderland F C 100–1
Sunley, JB 138
Sunningdale GC 15, 18–9, 101, 116

Sutherland Pilch, J 61, 64, 65–6, 80–1, 110
Sutton, T (Thomas) 9
Swanton, EW (cricket writer) 146
Sweetser, Jesse (US golfer) 99
Tanter, JB *132*
Tate, RD 71–2
Taylor, JD *132*
Taylor, JH (pro golfer) 18, 21, 39
Thatcher, Sir Denis *139*, 140
Thatcher, Lady Margaret *117*, 140
Thompson, JH 36–8, 42, 44, 46, 47–8, *50, 54, 89, 104*
Thompson, Jo 75
Thornton, R 138, 140
Tonbridge School 45, 56, 59, 66, 68–70
Travers, Ben 44, 47–8, 50, 53, **96–7**, 138, 143, *144*
Uppingham School 24, 80–1
Van Oss, O (Headmaster) 131
Very Senior B Darwin T'ment 92
Victoria, HM Queen 18, 19
Victoria of S-Holstein, Princess 18
Vogel, JLF 10–1, **114–5**
Walker Cup 60, 99, 102, 110, 112
Walton Heath GC 16, 23
Warner, Sir Pelham (cricketer/writer) 17
Watson's (George Watson's Coll) 22, *41, 45, 61, 63, 64–5, 69*
Weare FGC (Gerry) 36–8, 42, 44, 45–6, 49, *51, 52, 53–4, 89, 93, 95*, 115, 143

Weare AG (Ted) 52
Webster, Sir R see Alverstone
Wellington College 49, 54, 72, 131
Wethered, Joyce (golfer) 100
Wethered, RH 27
Whinney, HCD *50, 57, 93, 95*
Whitcombe, Charles (pro golfer) 39
White, CG 65
White, PHF 36, 40, 41–2, *43–4*, 46, *47–8*, 49
Whitgift School 60, 70–2
Wilkinson, SJC *132*
Williams, Col AE 27
Wilson, A R 131–2
Winchester College 33, 43, 47–8
Woking GC 127, 129
Woodbridge, CM (Cecil) 9–10, 11, 18
Woodbridge, CF (Cyril) 11, 16, 36, 38, 42, 44, *47*, 116
Woodhall Spa GC 127
Woolley, IR *90, 147*
Worplesdon GC 8 ,15, 118, 141
Wreford-Brown, AJ (Tony) 12, 65, 131
Wreford-Brown, Charles 10, 13
Wreford-Brown, Claude 12
Wreford-Brown, Rev G (Gerald) 13
Wreford-Brown, OE (Oswald) 10, 11
Wrefrord-Brown, Brig PE (Peter) 13, *57, 58, 79, 80, 89, 90*, 118
Wreford-Brown, Maj WH (William) 12
Wright, OAC *132*
Young, BMW (Headmaster) 143

Acknowledgements

The author wishes to thank the following for their kind permission to reproduce their copyright material images on the following pages: Andrew Murdoch p. 4; Barnaby Mote pp. 70, 72, 73, 74 (Hill), 77, 111, 120, 122, 125, 126, 154 (top), 155 (lower); Charterhouse Archives pp. 10, 11 (Davies), 12 (left), 13, 17, 19, 108, 114, 119, 132, 134, 135, 136/7, 138, 139 (photos), 140; *Golf World* (*Golf Illustrated*) pp. 14, 100; Hulton Archive/Getty Images pp. 28, 99; Kent County Cricket Club p. 98; Mary Evans Picture Library (*Bystander*) pp. 23, 40, 41, 101, 104, (lower) (*Tatler*) pp. 16, 27, 37, 38; RedJelly Studios p. 157; Roger Smeeton front cover, pp. 131(all), 41; Royal Mid-Surrey GC p. 116; Royal Cinque Ports GC pp. 26, 75 (top), 115; Sunningdale GC pp. 9, 19, 49.

Other images are from the private collections of members of OCGS and others, and are reproduced with their kind permission.

Every effort has been made to identify the source of copyright material. Where items have been obtained from archives or private collections or otherwise, it has often not been possible to track down the copyright holder.